CW01337732

SHACKLET
THE ANTARCTIC
and ENDURANCE

SHACKLETON

THE ANTARCTIC and ENDURANCE

edited by Jan Piggott

DULWICH COLLEGE

2000

This book is published on the occasion of the Exhibition *Shackleton: the Antarctic and Endurance* in the Old Library at Dulwich College. October 31, 2000 to 25 February, 2001

Published on the order of the Governors of Dulwich College, London SE21 7LD

Sponsored by CHRISTIE'S

EXHIBITION and CATALOGUE INFORMATION

Credit card orders: 00 44 + (0)20 8299 9222

Tel: 00 44 + (0)20 8299 9201
Fax: 00 44 + (0)20 8299 9245
Email: shackleton@dulwich.org.uk
Website: www.dulwich.org.uk/history/exhib_shack.htm

British Library Cataloguing-in-Publication Data
A CIP Record is available from The British Library

ISBN 0-9539493-0-3 (Cased)
ISBN 0-9539493-1-1 (Paperback)

Published by Dulwich College, London SE21 7LD

Edited by Dr. Jan Piggott, F.S.A., Keeper of Archives, Dulwich College
Designed and produced by David McLean

Printed in England by Battley Brothers, Clapham, London

Cover: Norman Wilkinson, *An Epic of the Sea* (details), Dulwich College.

Title-page: Frank Hurley, Leonard Hussey and his Dog Team, September 1915 (Royal Geographical Society).

Opposite: C. S. Jagger, *Sir Ernest Shackleton* (pictured in the sculptor's studio; the statue is now at the Royal Geographical Society, Kensington Gore, London SW7).

Contents

Foreword

Never before has there been an United Kingdom Exhibition wholly devoted to my grandfather, Ernest Shackleton. Never since his life-time has his reputation stood higher. Never, I do believe, will there be an Exhibition to surpass this one.

The commitment of the Master and Dulwich College, the talents of the Curator, the generosity of the sponsors and those who have lent – often for the first time – their precious objects, have all combined to produce this splendid result.

I am greatly honoured to have been asked to perform the Opening Ceremony.

Alexandra Shackleton

The Hon. Alexandra Shackleton

The Sir Ernest Shackleton Bursary

Dulwich College was founded in 1619 by Edward Alleyn, the famous Elizabethan actor-manager. His intention was to provide education for twelve poor scholars under the direction of a Master. Today Dulwich is a school of 1400, but over the centuries every effort has been made to fulfil the aim of the Founder and make a Dulwich education available to all boys, irrespective of wealth.

After the Second World War under my predecessor, the Master of the day, Christopher Gilkes, there developed what came to be known as the 'Dulwich Experiment' whereby over the years some 4,000 boys at Dulwich had their fees paid by Local Education Authorities. When that scheme came to an end, Central Government introduced Assisted Places at independent schools, and at one time over 300 boys here held such places. That scheme too is coming to an end.

In 1990 the Dulwich College Bursary Appeal was launched to try to raise money to enable boys to come to the College who would not otherwise, for financial reasons, be able to do so. To date, over £1.6m has been raised. Some of the Bursaries are 'named' after very generous donors, and I feel it would be fitting, as a tribute to arguably the College's most distinguished Old Boy, if there were to be at least one Sir Ernest Shackleton Bursary. I have, therefore, decided that half the proceeds from this Exhibition shall go towards establishing such a Bursary. I need hardly add that donations towards this Bursary would also be warmly welcomed.

I very much hope that you will enjoy the Exhibition.

Graham Able MA
Master of Dulwich College

Further details about the Dulwich College Bursary Appeal may be obtained from Terry Walsh, the Appeal Director, at the College.

Dulwich College is a Registered Charity, No. 312755

The Shackleton Scholarship Fund

Geologists, golf coaches, water-colour artists, sociologists, drummers, even a horse-whisperer – what could they have in common?

They are all among the thirty or so Shackleton Scholars who have visited the Falkland Islands and South Georgia in the five years since the Shackleton Scholarship Fund was established after the death of Edward, Lord Shackleton, in September 1994.

The Fund commemorates both Shackletons – Sir Ernest, the explorer and subject of this exhibition, who died in South Georgia in 1922 and his son Edward, also an explorer, but above all a statesman and a man of broad interests in government, industry and science. Both men were linked in different ways to the Falkland Islands – Sir Ernest used them as a base for his Antarctic expeditions and returned to their capital Stanley in 1916 after his extraordinary voyage across the Southern Ocean to bring help to his stranded party. Edward, Lord Shackleton, prepared two ground-breaking reports on the economic future of the Falkland Islands in 1977 and 1982 which mapped out the path of development and whose recommendations have been triumphantly justified by the Islands' remarkable prosperity since the 1982 conflict. In preparing these reports, Lord Shackleton developed a deep affection for the Islands and their people which they returned in full measure.

This explains the desire to create a living and permanent memorial to these two extraordinary men, and one which would strengthen the ties between the Falkland Islands and the rest of the world, and reduce the isolation which geography has imposed on the Islanders. The Shackleton Scholarship Fund is partly designed to promote post-graduate academic exchanges – hence the geologists and other scientists, the sociologists, the naturalists whose visits to the South Atlantic the Fund has backed. But it is more than that. The Fund also pays for visits by 'Quality of Life' scholars – people whose talents as performers or instructors are valued on the Islands but who could never pay for a trip south given the vast distances and the small audiences.

In all fifteen academic Scholars have visited the Islands, three Falkland Islanders have gone to places as diverse as Connecticut, New Zealand and South Georgia, and ten 'quality of life' Scholars have delighted audiences in Stanley, in camp (the countryside) and at the military bases. One couple combined both sorts of scholarship: Dr Kery Dalby is an expert on lichens; his wife Claire is an artist who has exhibited her paintings of the Islands on her return early this year.

Scholarships do not grow on trees: the Shackleton Scholarship Fund uses the income from a substantial capital sum raised after the memorial service for Lord Shackleton and placed under the aegis of the United Kingdom Falkland Island Trust. The Falkland Islands Government made the largest single contribution of £100,000, and companies and individuals in the Islands also proved outstandingly generous. In Britain and America those who had loved and admired the lives and work of Sir Ernest and his son also gave generously to the Fund. The capital sum raised, over £400,000, now finances around six visits south every year by both types of Scholar. Academic visits not only yield a rich harvest of research, papers and publications but also produce a greater understanding of the Islanders and their unique way of life; 'quality of life' scholars bring delight, new skills and new experiences to the people of the Islands.

The Fund is administered by two Committees: one in London which assesses and recommends academic scholars and one in Stanley which approves 'quality of life' proposals and takes the final decisions. Both committees welcome the decision to hold the Shackleton Exhibition at Dulwich College and are grateful that half of the sums raised will be devoted to Shackleton Scholarships. They welcome any additional donations from visitors to the Exhibition – donations in both Britain and the United States can enjoy favourable taxation status.

David Tatham,
Governor of the Falkland Islands
and Commissioner for South Georgia
and the South Sandwich Islands, 1992–95

Enquiries about the Shackleton Scholarship Fund from those wishing to contribute, or from post-graduate students seeking the Fund's support, should be directed to:

The Honorary Secretary
The Shackleton Scholarship Fund,
Falkland Islands Government Office,
14 Broadway, London SW1H 0BH

Tel: 020 7222 2542   Fax: 020 7222 2375

The Last Hurdle – following Shackleton's steps across South Georgia

Stephen Venables

The sun had already set when we reached the summit on the evening of January 21st 1990. Only a faint violet glow still lingered on the cloud froth spilling lazily over a mountain ridge that stretched seventy miles to the far north-western point of South Georgia. The air was still and the vast tracts of the Southern Ocean spread beneath us were utterly calm. It was one of those rare transcendental moments which a mountaineer never forgets, made special on this occasion because we had just made the first ascent of Mount Carse, named after the actor, broadcaster and polar explorer Duncan Carse. It was he who had masterminded a series of mapping expeditions to the island during the nineteen-fifties, unravelling the secrets of the mountain interior; but inevitably, standing on his summit, I also thought of the man who had crossed the mountains long before Carse made his map – the man whose name will always be associated with the island where he now lies buried – Ernest Shackleton.

From our summit we could just see the distant peaks where Shackleton, Worsley and Crean made their desperate traverse in 1916. We could also look down on the closer shore where they and their three companions were so nearly shipwrecked at the end of their fourteen day voyage in the *James Caird*. On this calm evening, looking out towards Anenkov Island, Jossac Bight, the Nunez Peninsula, Cape Rosa... all looking so benign, it was hard to imagine those six men in the *James Caird*, battered by hurricane force winds, deafened by the thunderous surf, bailing for their lives, fighting to keep the tiny boat afloat. It was only the next day, on our way back from Mount Carse, that I was reminded how unforgiving South Georgia can be. Caught offguard by violent katabatic winds funnelled down through a mountain pass, I was flung repeatedly from my skis and reduced eventually to crawling on hands and knees, blinded by wind-blasted particles of ice, until my companion came to the rescue, dragging me back to the safe haven of a snow cave.

It was a single, small, humbling incident, but it reinforced my admiration for what Shackleton and his crew achieved, making that perilous landfall in 1916. It also made me realize something of the courage – and extraordinary luck – which made possible their subsequent crossing of these wild and unpredictable mountains. Exploring the southern part of South Georgia had given me a feel for the place but I was inevitably curious to see for myself the north-western neck of the island, and follow the exact line of Shackleton's rescue mission from King Haakon Bay to Stromness. What was it really like – that final sting-in-the-tail of the most extraordinary escape story of all time?

My chance came ten years later, in April 2000, when I returned to South Georgia to take part in the IMAX film *Shackleton's Antarctic Adventure*, with two of the world's finest mountaineers. The thirty-seven-year old Californian Conrad Anker has pioneered some of the hardest climbs on the granite spires of Patagonia and Antarctica, along with some groundbreaking Himalayan ascents. In 1999, just before making an ascent of Everest, he discovered the body of George Mallory, where it had lain since 1924 at 27,000 feet above sea level. My other companion was Reinhold Messner, who was born and raised in the Dolomite mountains of South Tirol, where he achieved his first legendary climbs in the sixties, before going on to the Himalaya to redefine completely what was possible at high altitude. He was the first to climb Everest without oxygen, the first to solo Everest, and ultimately the first to climb all the fourteen 8000 metre peaks. In recent years he has been drawn from mountains to the emptiness of the polar icecaps and his own traverse of Antarctica was inspired by what Shackleton set out to attempt in 1914. At fifty-six he is universally acknowledged as the world's most influential mountaineer. His example certainly inspired my own Himalayan explorations, which have included a new route up the East Face of Everest, climbed without oxygen. At forty-six I was on my first expedition for a few years, thrilled to be returning to the fringes of Antarctica.

Aerial View of Crean Glacier, looking east towards the great dome-shaped nunatak
(Maria Stenzel/National Geographic Society Image Collection)

The plan was for the three of us to try and follow the exact route of Shackleton's traverse. Most of the filming was to be done at either end of the traverse, leaving the three of us unencumbered to cover the ground between as quickly as possible, travelling light. That way, we hoped to get an inkling of what it must have been like for the three men in 1916. Nevertheless, our approach to King Haakon Bay could not have been more different from Shackleton's in 1916. We were warm, comfortable and well fed aboard the polar research vessel, *Akademic Shulyekin*. And we were part of a large convivial team, including the American NOVA/WGBH Boston production team, the Canadian IMAX film crew, the director, George Butler, and the British field support team, Poles Apart. Again, it required a huge leap of the imagination to envisage the cramped, sodden, thirst-wracked torture aboard the *James Caird* on the sixteenth day as it slipped finally through the treacherous reef at the entrance to the bay.

We arrived on a dank drizzly morning. But as we steamed into King Haakon Bay the murk cleared and there were the jagged teeth of the reef, jostled by icebergs. And there, just inside the point of Cape Rosa

was the narrow cleft, overhung by festoons of tussock grass, where the men finally dragged their boat ashore, and fell to their knees to drink and drink and drink from a freshwater stream. As we steamed further into the bay I counted glaciers tumbling down onto the southern shore, trying unsuccessfully to make Shackleton's total of twelve, but much of the ice had retreated during the intervening eighty-four years. Nevertheless, it was still a formidable barrier and it was obvious that the route lay further east, over the pass now called Shackleton Gap.

King Haakon Bay is still only sketchily charted, so the captain anchored cautiously in the middle. From there we zoomed ashore in Zodiac inflatables, landing at Peggotty Bluff, where they made their final landing in 1916, turning the *James Caird* upside down for a makeshift Dickensian hut and building a huge fire from the driftwood which Worsley called 'a graveyard of ships'. With fresh water streams and green tussock, this spot must have seemed a luxurious oasis after the desolation of Elephant Island. I could imagine being tempted to linger, shrinking from the unknown mountains which still separated the men from the whaling stations on the north coast. I would have welcomed the three days stormy weather that pinned them down, as an excuse to delay action. But Shackleton was not like that. He was always fretting to be away, always initiating, leading from the front, facing the unknown with extrovert optimism, taking huge gambles because boldness offered the only possibility of success.

Of the six men, only three were still strong enough to attempt the mountain traverse. Vincent, the brawny bully, was utterly spent, as was McNeish, the carpenter without whose skills the *James Caird* would never have been made fit for her voyage. More surprising to me was the exhaustion of McCarthy, whose generous, ebullient, Irish humour had helped sustain them in the boat. But he too was all spent. Describing the departure from Peggotty Bluff, Worsley later wrote, 'how sad we should have been at parting with simple honest Timothy McCarthy, AB, had we known we should only see him once again for two days. He went down in the war, fighting his gun to the last, three short weeks after landing in England'.

But as yet they did not even know whether Europe was still at war. They had had no contact with the outside world since December 1914 and when Worsley, Crean and Shackleton set off at 3.00 am on May 16th 1916, they had no certainty of reaching the whaling stations safely. Shackleton, ever punctilious about firm delegation, left written instructions for the other three to survive off seals, birds and fish and concluded, 'in the event of my non-return you had better after winter is over try and sail round to the East Coast'. He had a rough idea where he was heading but knew nothing of the island's interior. In 1916 no-one had ever penetrated more than a mile or two inland. No-one had bothered to explore the glaciers, because there had been no need for it. The existing German coastal chart was at best sketchy and Worsley, that superlative navigator, had already, upon arriving in King Haakon Bay, had the dubious satisfaction of proving that it was positioned in the wrong place. In the absence of cartographic certainties, the three men were going to have to rely on canny intuition and their memories of the coastal landmarks they had seen seventeen months earlier when they set sail from South Georgia.

They had no knowledge of the land they had to cross nor were they equipped for a mountaineering expedition. The skis which would have aided them on the upper snowfields had long since been abandoned or vandalised for other purposes. For icy slopes they had only the salvaged woodscrews from the *James Caird*,

fixed to their bootsoles. For insulation Worsley and Crean had warm finneskoe, but Shackleton had characteristically given his pair to one of the men on Elephant Island keeping just thin leather boots for himself. For support they carried 'alpenstocks' fashioned out of sledging staves. In addition Shackleton carried a short-handled carpenter's adze for step-cutting and a short length of climbing rope. They also had a Primus stove and Nansen cooker and enough sledging rations to last a couple of days. But they had no tent and knew that in their tattered clothes and weakened condition they would not survive long in a blizzard. Shackleton's written description of the risks they faced is surprisingly terse, merely expressing the hope, soon to be shattered, that they would find tussock grass, not snow and ice. Worsley's florid depiction of the mountain perils, on the other hand, will resonate with anyone who has been subjected to a South Georgian blizzard: 'the hell that reigns up there in heavy storms…the wind fiends, thrown hissing, snarling, reverberating from crag to crag, from peak to precipice, hurtle revengefully on to the ice sheets, and calving, biting, gouging, tear out great chunks and lumps of ice to hurl them volcanically aloft…' And so on in full gothic flow. When the three men set off that still, moonlit night, they knew that it could not be long before the next storm hit South Georgia and that their only hope lay in speed.

We too set off in fine weather, eighty-four years later. After several hours filming, we started up the glacier in hot afternoon sunshine, the three of us accompanied by Mike Graber who was to take some video footage on the first part of the traverse. Shackleton Gap was shrouded in mist and we had to take a compass bearing to locate the tent pitched on the far side by the field support team. Soon after we arrived the cloud lifted to reveal water to the north. At night Shackleton mistook the sheen on this water for a great frozen lake and wasted at least an hour descending towards it before he saw the lapping of the sea swell. The existing chart was wildly inaccurate and he now realized that the island was extremely narrow at this point. He was descending towards Possession Bay. Although Captain Cook had made his historic landing here in 1775, there was no whaling station. The nearest station was further north, at Prince Olav Harbour but Shackleton was not at all sure, with midwinter approaching, that it would be manned, so he headed back up the glacier before bearing east towards the bigger station at Stromness.

How different it was for us, with our laminated copy of Duncan Carse's map. Give or take the odd detail, we

A sea view from the north of Possession Bay and the Murray Snowfield – the first big glacier crossed by Shackleton from right to left as he started the long eastward traverse towards Stromness. © Stephen Venables

knew exactly where we were going. Unlike the marine navigator Worsley, who consistently overestimated heights by a hundred percent, we knew the exact intervals involved. We also knew that the distance from Peggotty Camp to Stromness was twenty-three miles as the albatross flies and that the actual route taken by Shackleton was about thirty miles. We knew that other parties before us had repeated the route. One of the most recent, in 1999, had used skis and taken just twenty-nine hours, including a ten hour break forced by bad weather. The first ever repeat, by a British Services expedition in 1965, manhauling sledges through some atrocious weather, took nearly two weeks. One night a ski, left standing in the snow outside the tent, had its top half snapped off by the wind. Shackleton, doing the route on sight, without skis, travelling non-stop in a desperate last bid for rescue, took just thirty-six hours.

Time and time again in this great epic of the *Endurance* expedition, we find Shackleton treasuring every little shred of good fortune. In this final chapter he was extraordinarily lucky to have fine weather. But, where others might fritter away their luck, he used it to the utmost, forcing the pace, taking advantage of the additional bonus of a full moon. If anyone made and deserved their luck, he did. As soon as he realized the mistake with Possession Bay, he corrected the course and headed eastward across what is now called the Murray Snowfield. As the three men tramped over the undulating snow, now in full daylight, they began to understand the lie of the land. They were travelling almost due east, with the north coast to their left and the main mountain spine to their right. To complicate matters, this spine threw down spiky barriers north-

ward, blocking their path. As Worsley wrote afterwards, 'the snow upland over which we were travelling steepened ahead of us to a great ridge, through which five rocky crags, or nunataks, reared up like giant fingers, with what looked like passes between each pair'.

We reached these giant fingers at about midday on the first full day of our traverse after a late start from the first camp. Strong winds at dawn had prompted us to wait for a weather forecast. When the ship radioed through to say that the forecast was mediocre but not appalling, we decided to set off. Time was short and we might sit forever if we waited for perfect weather. Unlike Shackleton we had the portable security of a tiny bivouac tent for shelter and, more importantly, half the world knew where we were if something should go wrong.

So here we were, zigzagging our way up towards the first big obstacle, weaving a line through crevasses that had been covered in 1916. The four saddles were clearly visible and we could see how Shackleton was tempted to head for the right-hand, lowest one, cutting steps with the carpenter's adze. But when he got there, 'the outlook was disappointing. I looked down a sheer precipice to a chaos of crumpled ice 1500 feet below'. So back they went, before climbing up again, laboriously, to the second saddle. Again 'the same precipice confronted us'. They bypassed the third saddle and headed instead for the fourth and highest, skirting round the rim of a huge scoop, carved out of the glacier by the forces of wind and sun. In Worsley's account they arrived at the fourth gap, a razorback of ice, as darkness came on. The outlook here was not much better but Shackleton had run out of options. 'We could not see the bottom clearly owing to the mist and bad light, and the possibility of the slope ending in a sheer fall occurred to us; but the fog that was creeping up behind allowed no time for hesitation'. They started down carefully, roped together, cutting steps. Then, desperate to descend more quickly, they coiled the rope, sat down on it, clinging to each other's waists as they made a human toboggan shooting several hundred feet down the slope to the flat glacier below. 'We looked back up and saw the grey fingers of the fog appearing on the ridge, as though reaching after the intruders into untrodden wilds. But we had escaped'.

Yet again a bold gamble had saved the day. For us, 84 years later, there was not quite such urgency. Like the 1965 party we actually crossed by the third saddle, not the fourth. The 'finger' to its right looked like a miniature version of the Matterhorn. Below and to the left was Worsley's huge 'wind-carved chasm' that 'could easily have accommodated two battle cruisers'. With modern crampon spikes on our feet, we were able to climb quickly up to the saddle where we did some final video filming with Mike Graber, before saying good-bye and starting cautiously down the far side, towards what is now called the Crean Glacier.

Already in King Haakon Bay we had seen the drastic changes wrought by global warming. The glaciers have become mean, dessicated travesties of the great ice sheets which Shackleton traversed. If we had tried his fourth saddle we would have had an even harder time than we did descending from the third. As it was we barely found a route down. The whole slope was riven by gaping chasms; huge sections of ice had melted away to reveal vertiginous black rubble. Zigzagging backwards and forwards, edging over fragile snow-bridges, peering anxiously into blind alleys, we began to despair. At one point Reinhold announced in his thick Germanic accent, 'we are in a trap!' But a moment later he unroped and shot off down the slope shouting, 'but maybe I smell a way out!' With all the speed, skill and animal intuition that had made possible his legendary Himalayan climbs, he did succeed in nosing a way through. Moments later we saw him reappear far below, a tiny dot running across the flat surface of the Crean Glacier. Conrad and I followed his cunning track through a jumble of shattered ice blocks, hurrying down to the safety of the glacier. Looking back up at the slope taken by Shackleton, we could see that today a glissade would be quite suicidal.

That evening in 1916, exhilarated by the thrill of surviving their huge slide, the three men stopped to light the Primus stove and brew up a pot of 'hoosh'. Throughout the long march, as he had done throughout the boat journey, even under the most hideous conditions, Shackleton insisted religiously on regular hot drinks and meals. That determination always to keep stoking the calorie reserves of his men, seems to have been one of his greatest tricks as a leader. At a purely physical level, it kept the men well hydrated; also, as Worsley observed, 'we had trained mouths, gullets and stomachs until we could have swallowed food at almost boiling point, and so we got an extra degree of warmth into chilled and shivering bodies'. But more than that, the psychological boost of those regular restorative brewing sessions must have been incalculable.

Mindful of this, when we reached the end of our own descent, I hesitantly suggested that we might stop for a quick brew. The lean, fit, tall Californian looked as

though he could carry on forever. As for the Tyrolean veteran, he just announced, 'Unnecessary. We go on'. So we went on, me thirstily scooping up handfuls of icy glacial meltwater as I rushed along, trying to keep up with the others. At first the going was easy, following flat tongues of bare gritty ice, seamed by tiny, jumpable crevasses. But soon the crevasses began to widen. The little jumps became huge leaps. The tongues dwindled and we found ourselves in a labyrinth, with huge crevasses cutting the ice in both directions, slicing the glacier surface into a chequer board of giant cubes. Between cubes we jumped. Then on one gigantic leap Reinhold landed badly, cracking a bone in his right foot. As it was nearly dark I assumed that this might be a signal to stop and camp, while we assessed the situation. But, like Shackleton, Messner was not going to let a little pain get in his way. Once again, he announced, 'We go on'. Hobbling bravely, safeguarded by our short length of bootlace-thin kevlar rope, he climbed in and out of chasms for another hour at least until darkness forced us to stop and pitch our tiny tent on the top of a suitably flat cube.

After a long, thirsty day on the glaciers, there is nothing more comforting than the roar of the pressure stove, preparing the first of many pots of tea and soup. Reinhold had brought his favourite Antarctic ration – smoked ham which is ninety percent pure fat and dry Tyrolean bread. My contribution was a small flask of Calvados. Conrad had chocolate-coated coffee beans to get us moving the next morning, once Reinhold had stoically rammed his excruciatingly swollen foot back into its plastic boot. Then he set off bravely to do battle with the labyrinth.

Most of the parties who have repeated Shackleton's route have chosen the spring months of November and December, when the crevasses are still filled with winter snow. Travelling in the autumn month of April, we had to contend with bare ice. Only a month later, in May, Shackleton had been on snow virtually the whole way. Overall mean temperatures were probably lower in 1916, keeping the permanent snowline lower. Perhaps, also, there had been heavy autumn snowfall that year. That greater snow cover, combined with more extensive, less fractured, glaciation must account for the very different conditions Shackleton found. Where they were plodding over undulating snow, we had to teeter along ice blades, lower ourselves into deep turquoise caverns and slither through chimneys, all made excruciatingly painful for Reinhold with his broken foot. Without modern crampons and ice axes it

Conrad Anker and Reinhold Messner force follow a compass bearing. © Stephen Venables

would have been virtually impossible. As it was, the Crean Glacier occupied us for a total of ten and a half hours, whereas Shackleton covered the same ground in five hours, including 'hoosh' stops.

Shackleton's speed was on the face of it remarkable in the light of his apparent lack of mountaineering experience. One of the men left on Elephant Island, Thomas Hans Orde-Lees, commented afterwards in his diary: 'Shackleton admitted frequently that he was no mountaineer. How later, he, Worsley and Crean managed to cross South Georgia is an everlasting puzzle to me, none of the three had even as much training as Wordie and I'. This says a lot about the unpreparedness of British polar expeditions, in comparison to people like Amundsen. Orde-Lees was the only member of Shackeleton's team who took skiing seriously, for instance, and by his own admission he was not very good. However, perhaps he exaggerates the inexperience of the rescue party. Worsley had done a little climbing in the Alps. Shackleton and Crean, although not mountaineers as such, had priceless experience on the Antarctic mainland, including Shackleton's epic 1909 exploration of the Beardmore Glacier and Crean's prominent role in both of Scott's expeditions. They were hardly beginners at glacier travel.

They were also desperate men drawing on their deepest, instinctive reserves. And they were very lucky. After the big slide, as the three men continued across the Crean Glacier, fortune smiled once again on the team, as Worsley recalled: 'now a faint luminous glow showed behind… the ridge to the south-east, and we knew that our old dear friend, the moon, had not forgotten us'. Nevertheless, they had their problems, tramping along by moonlight. Frequently they were plagued by that glacial nightmare 'breakable crust', sinking in up their shins. 'We had been tramping for over sixteen hours [since leaving Peggotty]. Sir Ernest now made the halts about every twenty minutes and, as before, we spread-eagled on our backs for two minutes' rest'. Later that night, 'at eleven, near the great domed rock, we made hoosh'.

No hot brews for us, although my spartan companions did at least agree to a half hour halt at the most bizarre landmark of the entire route. From a distance it looked like a great overhanging 'glacial erratic' boulder, but as we drew close it materialised into the twisted wreckage of a huge Wessex helicopter, nose down in a crevasse. It had been slowly melting its way into the ice since it crashed here in the 1982 Falklands War, during a bungled attempt by the SAS to reconnoitre possible

Argentine defences at Stromness. As Conrad observed, sniffing the distinct tang of hydraulic fluid, still polluting the glacier after eighteen years, 'it makes a mockery of the ecologists telling us not to piss on the lichens'.

By now we had escaped the labyrinth and the surface was smooth. It was only on the final climb past the 'great domed rock' that we had to rope up for some dangerously fragile snow bridges spanning deep chasms. It was a cloudy afternoon when we reached the broad pass beside the rock. Unlike Shackleton we could not see all the way down to the 'large open bay' on the left. Looking down onto it at midnight, he hoped that it was Stromness Bay and the three men headed that way. As Shackleton recalled later, 'I suppose our desires were giving wings to our fancies, for we pointed out joyfully various landmarks revealed by the now vagrant light of the moon, whose friendly face was cloud-swept. Our high hopes were soon shattered. Crevasses warned us that we were on another glacier'.

He remembered bitterly that no glacier descends into Stromness Bay and that they had only reached Fortuna Bay. Fearful of the chaotic icefall tumbling into the bay, they retraced their steps, to find an alternative way round the head of the bay. For Worsley 'this was the weariest part of the whole journey, partly no doubt from the hopeless feeling at having to retrace our steps and climb again to previously hard-won heights'.

The captain then mentions how the rope sometimes went slack – a familiar irritant to any seasoned glacier traveller. 'But,' he goes on, 'with fatigued men it is almost more than they can bear if it happens often and, following the example of our leader, we all did our utmost to help and consider each other and avoid any cause of annoyance, however trivial. Responding to Shackleton's unselfishness, teamwork was pulling us through. Although Crean and I had several times asked him to let us take the lead for a while, he would not, but led the whole journey, though it was certainly more exhausting breaking the trail, and I thought I could see it telling on him, yet he kept as cheery as ever. In normal times he would sometimes be irritable, but never when things were going badly and we were up against it'.

It was soon after this, at dawn, over twenty four hours after leaving Peggotty, that Shackleton pulled yet another trick out of his leadership bag. It was 5.00 am and they were just below yet another ridge, heading for a gap 'like a missing tooth'. The men were moving like automatons, barely able to put one foot in front of the other so Shackleton suggested a quick rest. Despite the cold the other two fell immediately into an exhausted sleep, but Shackleton resisted the temptation to relax, staying awake instead to watch over them. After five minutes, he shook them awake and told them that they had slept for half an hour. Transformed by that psychological boost they followed him up the final steep slope to the gap, which they reached just after 6.00 am.

Now, at last, after all those months on the floating ice, all those narrow escapes, the miserable landing on Elephant Island, the days of torture in the boat and these last hours of uncertain struggle on the glaciers, they saw their Ithaca. Immediately below them,

Conrad Anker and Reinhold Messner negotiating a crevasse on the descent to Fortuna Bay, towards the end of the traverse. Shackleton, arriving here in the middle of the night, dared not descend this broken glacier and tongue and retraced his steps to cross a high ridge further north. © Stephen Venables

The view down to Stromness from the last pass. When Shackleton, Crean and Worsley were here on May 17th 1916, there was snow under-foot. The buildings of Stromness had not been reddened by rust, the bay was filled with ships and they could even make out little human figures moving about the station – the first people from the outside world they had seen for seventeen months. © Stephen Venables

penguins strutted on the beach of Fortuna Bay, redolent of life and hope. But the real thrill was to see beyond Fortuna to the far side of a low range of hills, where they caught 'glimpses of the water of Stromness Bay – our goal'. This time, wrote Worsley, there was no mistaking it: 'Sir Ernest recognized a remarkable Z-shaped stratification of the great rocky face on the far side of Stromness Bay, and we felt that we were safe'. But the moment in the odyssey which really makes one's hairs stand on end with emotion comes a little later, as they stop for breakfast 'hoosh'. At 7.00 am precisely, on the dot of the ship's chronometer which they had carried all the way from the wreck of the *Endurance*, they heard the unmistakable sound of the Stromness steam-whistle summoning the whalers to work. 'Never,' wrote Shackleton, 'had any of us heard sweeter music. It was the first sound created by outside human agency that had come to our ears since we left Stromness Bay in December 1914'. It was now May 20th 1916. For the second time on the crossing of South Georgia (the first was at the foot of the big slide) the three men shook hands.

Our pilgrimage had to miss out the gapped ridge. Having taken a full day to escape the Crean Glacier labyrinth and pass the domed rock, we camped on the Fortuna Glacier. Then on the third full day of our traverse, we cheated a little, following Shackleton's abortive route down towards the tongue of the glacier, where the field support team had discovered a dry valley leading down past the icefall, perhaps not there in 1916, or at least not easily seen by moonlight. Our excuse was that Reinhold's foot was now excruciatingly swollen. By avoiding the laborious climb up and over the toothgap ridge, we increased his chances of reaching Stromness in time for the filming scheduled for that afternoon.

So we never witnessed the steep slope where, soon after hearing the distant factory whistle, Shackleton adopted an eccentric mountaineering technique, lying on his back and reaching down with his adze to cut steps. Nevertheless, even with our alternative route, it was an exhilarating morning, starting in a swirling maelstrom on the glacier. Buffeted by the wind, prodding the surface for hidden crevasses, groping through the clouds of spindrift, we got a taste of what South Georgia could produce. But it was only a brief taste. By midday we were walking round the beach of Fortuna Bay in warm sunshine, overtaking the shuffling throng of indignant penguins. Skimming the emerald hillside above, a pair of light-mantled sooty albatrosses danced their incomparable aerial ballet.

We raced round the head of the bay, where Conrad took the lead on a barefoot, thigh-deep wade of the icy river which flows out of the König Glacier. Then it was back on with socks and boots for one more climb. After the tortuous glaciers, this final ridge was a joyful, light-hearted affair of springy turf with a serene little tarn just below the final pass. How different from May 1916, when the imperfectly frozen pool was smothered in snow, tempting Shackleton with the relief of its flat surface, until he found himself sinking into the mush. Even this lower ridge tested to the limits the resolve of those three men, who must by now have been living off distilled adrenalin.

Although they had already heard the whistle and glimpsed Stromness Bay, they had not yet actually *seen* the whaling station. So perhaps the greatest moment of all was this final pass, which they reached at 1.30pm. We were a little later in the afternoon and of course there were no sailing ships moving in the bay, no 'minute figures moving to and fro'. But the buildings were still there, rust-mellowed to a rich russet, glowing against the turquoise bay, with those unmistakable swirling z-shaped rocks on the distant hillside. With no snow to confuse us, we managed to avoid the deceptive slope that led Shackleton down through his final test – an abseil through a half-frozen waterfall. Our descent into Stromness was gentler. Only three days stubble darkened our jaws and our colourful Polartec clothes seemed embarrassingly clean. How different from the three tattered, hairy men, blackened by the engrained soot of countless seal blubber fires, who tramped into the whaling station, carrying just an adze, cooker and the ship's log. 'That,' wrote Shackleton, 'was all, except our wet clothes, that we had brought out of the Antarctic, which we had entered a year and a half before with well-found ship, full equipment and high hopes. That was all of tangible things; but in memories we were rich. We had pierced the veneer of outside things. We had "suffered, starved, and triumphed, grovelled down yet grasped at glory, grown bigger in the bigness of the whole". We had seen God in his splendours, heard the text that Nature renders. We had reached the naked soul of man'.

Few, if any, explorers have survived adventures as remarkable as Shackleton's, yet for all of us – and not just explorers – those words resonate deeply. His story is universal because we all wonder how we would have coped if we had been there – wonder, whether we would, like Shackleton, Worsley and Crean on that final supreme test, have grown in stature. Of the three of us who followed their steps in April 2000, even Reinhold Messner had not experienced anything quite so cathartic as Shackleton's rescue mission. But we had all had our difficult moments on Himalayan expeditions. Retracing his steps across South Georgia, experiencing for ourselves the complexity of that difficult mountainous country which he crossed so rapidly, with only the haziest knowledge of what he would find, and no proper mountaineering equipment, we were all filled with intense, almost incredulous, admiration for what he achieved.

Notes

Quotations are made from Ernest Shackleton, *South*, 1919, chapter X, and Frank Worsley, *Shackleton's Boat Journey*, (1940), Part II, 'Crossing South Georgia'. See also Alfred Lansing, *Endurance*, 1959, Part VII, Chapters 1–2. The quotation from T. H. Orde-Lees' diary is from p. 3 of a typescript at the end of the section of his manuscript diary in Dartmouth College Library, Hanover, New Hampshire.

Shackleton's Antarctic Adventure, due in IMAX theatres in February 2001, is a co-production of White Mountain Films and NOVA/WGBH Boston, and is a presentation of Morgan Stanley Dean Witter.

Shackleton and the 'Heroic Age' of Antarctic Exploration

R. K. Headland
Scott Polar Research Institute

The connexion between Sir Ernest Henry Shackleton and the 'Heroic Age' of exploration in the Antarctic is one of the strongest. It may be described by an introductory note following his progress during four expeditions beginning in 1901 and ending with his untimely death in the Antarctic in 1922.

Greater detail of Shackleton's biography is given elsewhere in this publication. His ancestry was mixed, from Ireland and northern England, where both sides had significant maritime and colonial traditions. A biographer, Hugh Mill, suggested that this may account for the mingling of caution, perseverance, reckless courage, and strong idealism which were his leading characteristics.[1]

The 'Heroic Age' of Antarctic exploration is a reasonably well-defined historical period that began in the 1890s and ended just after the First World War. Prior to it Antarctica was very much the unknown continent with barely 25 scientific expeditions having seen it, although it has an area larger than that of Europe. The 'Heroic Age' had two origins: a practical one and a theoretical one from 1895. The practical beginning of this 'Heroic Age' was: three Norwegian whaling reconnaissances to the Antarctic Peninsula and Ross Sea regions; and a British whaling expedition from Dundee.[2]

The theoretical origin was sixth International Geographical Congress in London organized by the Royal Geographical Society. This finished on 3 August 1895 when a resolution was presented:

> That this congress record its opinion that the exploration of the Antarctic Regions is the greatest piece of geographical exploration still to be undertaken. That in view of the additions to knowledge in almost every branch of science which would result from such a scientific exploration the Congress recommends that the scientific societies throughout the world should urge in whatever way seems to them most effective, that this work should be undertaken before the close of the century.[3]

This resolution was adopted unanimously.

During this 'Heroic Age' expeditions to winter in Antarctica were dispatched from Argentina, Australia, Belgium, Britain, France, Germany, New Zealand, Norway, and Sweden. Summer expeditions were also dispatched from these countries and from Chile, Japan, and Uruguay while commercial voyages also arrived from Canada, Newfoundland, South Africa, and the United States.

The 'Heroic Age' included the beginnings of the modern whaling industry which, for good or bad,

1. *Eva* the hydrogen balloon from *Discovery*, 4 February, 1902. The first flight was by Scott, the second by Shackleton.

became the next dominant factor in Antarctic history. During this time public interest in Antarctica was very strong. The earliest winterings were made south of the Antarctic Circle (1898, aboard *Belgica*) and on Antarctica (1899, at Cape Adare). The last of the peri-Antarctic islands was discovered (Scott Island in 1902) and the general limits of Antarctica became known during this period. The South Pole was reached twice in the 1911–12 summer (33 days separated these events). The earliest Antarctic sound recordings were made in 1902 and successful cinematograph films in 1908. Twice in 1902 aircraft (balloons) were used for aerial reconnaissance (fig. 1). Radio communications were established between Antarctica and Australia in 1912, through a relay station on Macquarie Island. In 1903 the first permanent meteorological station was opened (on the South Orkney Islands) and in 1904 the first shore whaling station was established (on South Georgia). Coincidentally at least seventeen determined, but unsuccessful, attempts to reach the North Pole were made during this brief, but intense, period. The following summary, *Principal Expeditions during the Heroic Age of Antarctica*, gives very concise details of the expeditions of the age and their accomplishments in 'unveiling the Antarctic'.

Shackleton's earliest introduction to Antarctica was as a member of the British National Antarctic Expedition of 1901–04 led by Robert Falcon Scott aboard *Discovery* which made the first extensive land exploration of Antarctica. His desire for adventure, not unmixed with hope of fame, led him to apply for a post after the expedition was announced. At first this was unsuccessful as the Royal Navy and Merchant Marine were not fully compatible, and there were a few other problems. His experience with sailing vessels was, however, a strong point in his favour. On eventual appointment he was described as 'more intelligent than the average officer. His brother officers considered him to be a very good fellow, always quoting poetry and full of erratic ideas'.[4]

Discovery reached McMurdo Sound in February 1902 and wintered off Hut Point, Ross Island, for two years. Much exploration was accomplished including several major inland treks, the earliest deep penetration of the interior. During the winter a magazine, *The South Polar Times*, was produced, edited by Shackleton. Today such a tradition continues as most modern Antarctic stations produce a mid-winter magazine.

During the second summer a sledge party of three, Scott, Shackleton, and Edward Wilson reached a new

farthest south 82·28° S on 30 December 1902. This was at Shackleton Inlet, towards the foot of the Beardmore Glacier, the route to the pole up which all three men would later pass. Shackleton returned from this traverse greatly debilitated, mainly a result of incipient scurvy. This caused Scott to send him, with some others, home aboard the relief ship *Morning* during the 1902–03 summer. Thus he spent only the 1902 winter in Antarctica.

The *Discovery* expedition reinforced Shackleton's passion for Antarctica. He wrote, 'The stark polar lands grip the hearts of the men who have lived on them in a manner that can hardly be understood by the people who have never got outside the pale of civilization'.[5]

During this early part of the 'Heroic Age' another expedition set out from Britain: the Scottish National Antarctic Expedition of 1902–04 led by William Bruce aboard *Scotia*. Among its many accomplishments was the establishment of a meteorological observatory on the South Orkney Islands, on 1 April 1903, which is still

2. Omond House, South Orkney Islands, 22 February, 1904; the station being transferred by William Bruce to the Argentine Ministry of Agriculture.

3. Grytviken whaling station in 1914; Shackleton's 'Gateway to the Antarctic'.

open (fig. 2). After Bruce returned to Edinburgh in 1904 he started planning a trans-Antarctic expedition to set out in 1911 but insufficient finance made this impossible. Shackleton was involved from the beginning and was able to advance the concept enormously.[6]

Although not exploratory, Carl Larsen from Norway, who had already made three Antarctic voyages, established the first Antarctic whaling station at Grytviken on South Georgia in 1904. This made the island an important forward base for exploration, referred to by Shackleton as *the gateway to Antarctica*, and for several expeditions the whalers also provided a safety net (fig. 3).

By 1905 these expeditions had accomplished what was effectively the first portion of the 'Heroic Age' expeditions which, although making many major discoveries, raised more questions. It also reinforced the continuing strong impetus for Antarctic exploration which caused the age to continue for a second portion with further research and discovery.

The fulfilment of one of Shackleton's Antarctic ambitions was an expedition to explore a new region. In August 1907 he sailed in command of his second expedition which was productive in much exploration and research: the position of the South Magnetic Pole was reached, the volcano Mount Erebus was climbed, and numerous scientific programmes were undertaken. Shackleton led a journey intending to reach the South Pole. The party of four ascended the Beardmore Glacier where they discovered the Polar Plateau and set out across it. A farthest south was reached on 9 January 1909 at 88.38°S. Here Shackleton determined that the South Pole could be reached but that food and fuel

were insufficient to ensure the safe return of the party; thus he retreated. His calculations were proven correct; the party barely managed to survive the journey. His decision involved four lives and he commented later 'death lay ahead and food behind, so I had to return'.[7]

On his return to Britain Shackleton was knighted and received other awards. His remark to his wife demonstrated a justifiable respect for survival: 'I thought you'd rather have a live donkey than a dead lion'. For the press he commented more practically that 'with another 25 pounds of biscuits and 30 pounds of pemmican' they could have attained the pole.[8] This was perhaps consoling, it was certainly dramatic, and it was probably true (fig. 4).

The *Nimrod* expedition was also innovative; the earliest attempt to use a motor vehicle was made, but without significant success; a book, *Aurora Australis* was printed, even Antarctic postage stamps were issued, but more for revenue than for postage (a circumstance that certainly prevails today). The base hut at Cape Royds remains, one of those very well maintained by the New Zealand Antarctic Heritage Trust.

Another exceptional burst of Antarctic exploration occurred in 1910 and 1911 when five expeditions set out from Norway, Japan, Britain, Australia, and Germany. Other Antarctic visitors were the regular voyages of whalers to South Georgia, Iles Kerguelen, the South Shetland Islands, and elsewhere, as well as the annual Argentine supply voyage to the South Orkney Islands.

Roald Amundsen aboard *Fram* had originally planned a North Pole expedition but, after believing the false claims that this had been attained, he covertly changed his object. The expedition wintered at the Bay of Whales, Ross Ice Shelf, from where, after one false start, five men reached the South Pole on 14 December 1911 by dog sledge. On passing Shackleton's farthest south Amundsen wrote:

> We did not pass that spot without according our highest tribute to the man, who – together with his gallant companions – had planted his country's flag so infinitely nearer to the goal than any of his precursors. Sir Ernest Shackleton's name will always be written in the annals of Antarctic exploration in letters of fire. Pluck and grit can work wonders, and I know of no better example of this than what that man has accomplished.[9]

In Britain, and many other countries, the last expedition of Robert Falcon Scott aboard *Terra Nova* remains one of the best known. Another hut was established on Ross Island from where, after wintering,

4. Shackleton's farthest south, 9 January, 1909.

5. Captain Scott's expedition finding Captain Amundsen's *Polheim* tent at the South Pole, 17 January, 1912.

five men also reached the South Pole, arriving on 17 January 1912 by man-hauling (fig. 5). There they found Amundsen's expedition had departed 33 days previously; all five perished during the return journey. The story of the tragedy, with magnificent paintings and photographs, brought back by the survivors, served to concentrate more attention on Antarctica.[10]

In 1911 Wilhelm Filchner departed on a German South Polar Expedition aboard *Deutschland*. This was planned to make a continental traverse but lack of funds reduced the ambitions. After South Georgia *Deutschland* continued south to the Luitpold Coast of the Weddell Sea where an attempt to establish a station was unsuccessful because of ice conditions. *Deutschland* became beset and drifted in pack ice for nine months but her course did not take her into the mills of ice which crushed the Swedish ship *Antarctic* in 1903 and which were to crush *Endurance*.[11] The year 1911 was also the year of departure of the Australasian Antarctic Expedition led by Douglas Mawson aboard *Aurora*. Mawson had served with Shackleton during the *Nimrod* expedition.

With the strong interest in Antarctic exploration and the vast amount of land discovered, Shackleton then began to plan his third and most ambitious expedition: the crossing of Antarctica. It involved two parties aboard two vessels: *Endurance* in the Weddell Sea which he led, and *Aurora* in the Ross Sea led by Æneas Mackintosh. The expedition left London in 1914, a year with exceptional ice conditions around Antarctica. Both vessels got into severe difficulties. *Endurance* reached South Georgia, where the whalers gave warnings of severe ice, thence continued into the Weddell Sea where she became beset and drifted like *Deutschland* but closer to the coast and was caught in the mills of ice off the Antarctic Peninsula, was crushed and sank. The

narration of the consequences with travel over unstable ice, taking to small boats, reaching Elephant Island, preparation of *James Caird*, the voyage to South Georgia, traverse to a whaling station, and ultimate rescue of all those on Elephant Island, is an exceptional epic of survival. Perhaps one more quotation might serve to illustrate the circumstances. Leaving behind everything unnecessary so that individual loads weighed only two pounds, Shackleton wrote: 'A man under such conditions needs something to occupy his thoughts, some tangible memento of his home and people beyond the seas. So sovereigns were thrown away and photographs were kept'.[12]

On arriving at Stromness whaling station on South Georgia in May 1916, Frank Worsley described the party as 'ragged, filthy, evil-smelling; hair and beards long and matted with soot and blubber; unwashed for three months, and no bath nor change of clothing for seven months'.[13] Shackleton continued, 'Down we hurried, and when quite close to the station we met two small boys about ten or twelve years of age. I asked these lads where the manager's house was situated. They did not answer. They gave us one look – a comprehensive look that did not need to be repeated. Then they ran from us as fast as their legs could carry them... We met an old man, who started as if he had seen the Devil himself and gave us no time to ask any question. He hurried away'. On arriving at the Manager's Villa they met the steward who left them outside, perhaps a necessary precaution, and announced, 'There are three funny-looking men outside who say they have come over the island and know you'. The manager came to the door and said, 'Well?' Shackleton responded, 'Don't you know me?' and after it was obvious he had not been recognized added, 'My name is Shackleton'.[14] The welcome was then immediate, followed by baths. Shackleton immediately started to organize rescue attempts from South Georgia, the Falkland Islands, Uruguay, Chile and Britain. The fourth, aboard *Yelcho* from Chile, was successful. All the men returned alive.

On the other side of Antarctica the fate of the Ross Sea party was less providential. *Aurora* was blown out in a blizzard and caught in drifting pack-ice, eventually reaching New Zealand seriously damaged. The stranded land party, with minimal supplies, laid depots for the expected but non-existent, crossing party. Three died and the survivors were not rescued until 1917.[15]

It was not until 1958 that a traverse across Antarctica, such as planned by Bruce and Filchner, and attempted by Shackleton, was successful. This was the Commonwealth Trans-Antarctic Expedition led by Sir Vivian Fuchs.

Shackleton's specialisations resulted in him becoming involved in various Arctic operations during the first World War, particularly in Murmansk. This, with his polar interests and the desire for a survey of part of the Canadian Arctic, led to him making arrangements for a northern expedition aboard *Quest*, a Norwegian sealing vessel. At a late stage there was a change of government in Canada which led to the cancellation of the Arctic survey. This left Shackleton with an almost complete polar expedition and nowhere to go. The situation was resolved by a private contributor, thus the Shackleton-Rowett Expedition departed from London for the Antarctic in September 1921; Shackleton's fourth Antarctic expedition.[16]

The objects were several, including investigation of several peri-Antarctic islands. *Quest* made a slow journey south, South Georgia was reached on 4 January 1922 after a rough passage. Early in the morning of 5 January Shackleton died of a heart attack. The second in command, Frank Wild, decided that Shackleton's desire in such circumstances would have been to proceed; thus in as far as practicable, the expedition continued its scientific programme.

Shackleton's body was interred in the whalers' and sealers' cemetery at King Edward Cove, on South Georgia. In 1928 a granite monument was erected over it which bore a quotation from Robert Browning: 'I hold that a man should strive to the uttermost for his life's set prize'.

There has always been questioning of the significance and motives of the explorations, of revisionism, of scurrilous interpretations, of excess heroics, of scholarship, and of other issues which, at least, ensure that the 'Heroic Age' remains familiar. Regarding leadership, a particularly apt observation was made by Apsley Cherry-Garrard in the preface to *The Worst Journey in the World*. It goes:

> What is the use of A running down Scott because he served with Shackleton, or B going for Amundsen because he served with Scott ? They have all done good work; within their limits, the best work to date. There are jobs for which, if I had to do them, I would like to serve under Scott, Amundsen, Shackleton and Wilson – each to his part. For a joint scientific and geographical piece of organization, give me Scott; for a Winter Journey, Wilson; for a dash to the Pole and nothing else, Amundsen: and if I am in a devil of a hole and want to get out of it, give me Shackleton every time. They will all go down in history as leaders, these men.[17]

Notes

1   H. R. Mill, *The Life of Sir Ernest Shackleton*, 1924, p. 290.
2   R. K. Headland, *Chronological List of Antarctic Expeditions and Related Historical Events*, Cambridge, 1989.
3   J. S. Keltie and H. R. Mill, *Report of the Sixth International Geographical Congress*, 1896, p. 780.
4   M. & J. Fisher, *Shackleton*, 1957, p. 23.
5   Ibid., p. 218.
6   W. S. Bruce, 'A New Scottish Expedition to the South Polar Regions', Edinburgh, *Scottish Geographical Journal*, 24 (4), 1908, pp. 200–202.
7   Fisher, p. 218.
8   Fisher, p. 219.
9   R. E. G. Amundsen, *The South Pole*, 1912, II, p. 114.
10   L. Huxley, (ed.), *Scott's Last Expedition*, 1913.
11   W. Filchner, *Zum sechsten Erdteil. Die zweite Deutsche Südpolar Expedition*, 1922, Berlin.
12   Ernest Shackleton, *South*, 1919, p. 83.
13   F. Worsley, *Shackleton's Boat Journey*, 1940, p. 181.
14   Shackleton, 1919, p. 206.
15   R. W. Richards, *The Ross Sea Shore Party*, Cambridge, 1962.
16   F. Wild, *Shackleton's Last Voyage*, 1923.
17   Apsley Cherry-Garrard, *The Worst Journey in the World*, 1922, p. vii.

Principal Expeditions
during the 'Heroic Age' of Antarctica

R. K. Headland
Scott Polar Research Institute

This extract is from: Headland, R. K. 2000 (October). *Antarctic Chronology*. Unpublished revision of *Chronological List of Antarctic Expeditions and Related Historical Events*. Cambridge University Press, 1989

1892–93 British whaling exploration (from Dundee)

Alexander Fairweather	*Balaena*
Thomas Robertson	*Active*
Robert Davidson	*Diana*
James Davidson	*Polar Star*

Pioneer Scottish whaling reconnaissance, the Dundee whaling fleet, visited the Falkland Islands;

William Speirs Bruce (*Balaena*) and Charles W. Donald (*Active*) undertook some scientific work in the Joinville Island group and northern Trinity Peninsula; Robertson discovered and roughly charted Active Sound and the Firth of Tay; William Gordon Burn Murdoch, an artist, accompanied the expedition aboard *Balaena*. No whales were successfully caught but a large quantity of seal skins and oil (presumably Crab-eater Seals) were obtained. The fleet met Carl Anton Larsen aboard *Jason*, near Joinville Island, 24 December 1892. The earliest known photographs of Antarctica were taken during this expedition.

1892–93 Norwegian whaling exploration (from Sandefjord)

Carl Anton Larsen	*Jason*

Pioneer whaling reconnaissance; raised Norwegian flag, 4 December 1892, and collected fossils on Seymour Island; penetrated Weddell Sea to 64·67° S, 56·50° W, reporting an 'appearance of land' to the west of this position; visited the South Orkney Islands. Larsen met the Dundee whaling fleet near Joinville Island, 24 December 1892.

1893–94 Norwegian sealing and whaling exploration (from Sandefjord)

Carl Anton Larsen	*Jason*
Morten Pedersen	*Castor*
Carl Julius Evensen	*Hertha*

Visited the South Shetland Islands. *Hertha* sailed south between the Biscoe Islands and the Antarctic Peninsula to 69·17° S, sighted Adelaide Island, Hugo Island, and Alexander Island. *Hertha* and *Castor* sailed in company to meet *Jason* at South Georgia. Whale harpooned from *Hertha*, but lost, in Royal Bay, 20 April 1894. Larsen discovered King Oscar II Coast, Foyn Coast, and Robertson Island (reported a volcanic eruption at Seal Nunataks); penetrated Weddell Sea coast of the Antarctic Peninsula to 68·17° S, and made first use of ski in Antarctica; visited the South Orkney Islands and Falkland Islands. Jason met the other vessels at Jason Harbour, South Georgia. The expedition secured 13,223 seal skins (presumably Crab-eater Seals from near the Antarctic Peninsula) and 6600 barrels (1.1 x 106 litres) of seal oil. [Larsen wrote to the Royal Geographical Society, London, inquiring about leasing South Georgia as a site for a whaling station, February 1896.]

1893–95 Norwegian sealing and whaling exploration (from Tønsberg)

Henrik Johan Bull (Leader)	
Leonard Kristensen	*Antarctic*

Dispatched by Svend Foyn to investigate Antarctic whaling possibilities. Visited Tristan da Cunha, sighted Prince Edward Islands and Iles Crozet, took Elephant Seals on Iles Kerguelen, sighted Macquarie Island, visited the Auckland Islands and Campbell Island during winter 1894, sighted Balleny Islands; landed on Possession Island in the Ross Sea, and at Cape Adare where raised the Norwegian flag, 24 January 1895 (the second landing on Victoria Land, and probably the sixth on mainland Antarctica). Searched for non-existent 'Royal Company Island' and 'Emerald Island'.

1895 Sixth International Geographical Congress
meeting in London adopted a resolution (number 3)

at its closing session, 3 August, 'That this congress record its opinion that the exploration of the Antarctic Regions is the greatest piece of geographical exploration still to be undertaken. That in view of the additions to knowledge in almost every branch of science which would result from such a scientific exploration the Congress recommends that the scientific societies throughout the world should urge in whatever way seems to them most effective, that this work should be undertaken before the close of the century'.

1897–99 Belgian Antarctic Expedition

Adrien Victor Joseph de Gerlache
de Gomery *Belgica*

Visited the South Shetland Islands; explored the eastern part of Bismarck Strait; discovered and mapped Gerlache Strait and Danco Coast; named Palmer Archipelago; sighted Alexander Island. *Belgica* was beset by pack ice and drifted south of Peter Iøy for 12 months, the first exploring vessel to winter in the Southern Ocean and first men (18) wintering south of the Antarctic Circle; visited Tierra del Fuego. Two men died off the Antarctic Peninsula.

1898–99 German Deep Sea Expedition

Carl Chun
Adalbert Krech *Valdivia*

Oceanographic voyage in Indian and Atlantic Oceans; visited Bouvetøya (and accurately fixed its position for the first time), Iles Kerguelen, Ile Saint-Paul, and Ile Amsterdam. Met Elysée Hermann and his family living on Ile Saint-Paul, running a fishing enterprise with the vessel *H. B. P.*

1898–1900 British Antarctic Expedition

Carsten Egeberg Borchgrevink
Bernhard Jensen *Southern Cross*

Visited the Balleny Islands (reported an eruption), examined a large stretch of coast of Victoria Land; landed at Cape Adare and raised the British flag, 2 March 1899; built 2 huts where 10 men wintered ('Camp Ridley', the first party to do so on Antarctica (*Southern Cross* wintered in New Zealand); examined the Ross Ice Shelf, sledging party reached a farthest south of 78·83°, 23 February 1900; used dogs and kayaks for transport (first use in Antarctica); established a mid-winter camp, 'Stone Hut', on Duke of York Island where made another territorial claim. Nicolai Hanson (Norway), zoologist, died, 14 October

1899, and was buried at Cape Adare. On the return voyage visited the Auckland Islands and Macquarie Island. Scientific investigations included zoology, geology, meteorology, and terrestrial magnetism; ciné pictures attempted unsuccessfully. By prior arrangement *Carin*, from Melbourne, awaited *Southern Cross* at Campbell Island with stores but missed her, 1 February to 21 March 1899. [The expedition included 2 Lapps, Ole Must and Persen Savio, employed as dog handlers. Borchgrevink was a Norwegian, resident in Australia; he organized the expedition in Britain with private patronage, later he applied for United States citizenship.]

1901–03 German Deep Sea Expedition

Erich Dagobert von Drygalski
Hans Ruser *Gauss*

Gauss, with a complement of 32 was beset and wintered in the Antarctic pack ice (about 80 km offshore); expedition discovered Wilhelm II Land and sledged to Gaussberg; visited Iles Crozet, Heard Island (investigated glaciation), Ile Saint-Paul, and Ile Amsterdam. Made 3 ascents in a tethered hydrogen balloon at winter quarters, 29 March 1902, reached 480 m altitude and relayed observations the ship by telephone. Made sound recordings of birds on Edison cylinders, used an electric lighting system, and made diving observations from the ship in the ice. Separate scientific party of 6 men, under Emil Werth, spent 16 months on Iles Kerguelen, 1902–03, with support vessels *Tanglin* (Kapt. Neuhaus), Duisburg (Kapt. Brunhs), *Stassfurt* (Kapt. Wommelsdorf), and *Essen*, sheep introduced. An outbreak of beri-beri caused two deaths aboard *Tanglin*, another man died in Iles Kerguelen. At the conclusion of the expedition sledge dogs were freed on Iles Kerguelen, they became feral and their progeny persisted until at least 1929.

1901–04 Swedish South Polar Expedition

Nils Otto Gustaf Nordenskjold
Carl Anton Larsen *Antarctic*

Shore party of 6 men wintered on Snow Hill Island; proved Dumont d'Urville's 'Louis Philippe Land' (now Trinity Peninsula) to be a part of the Antarctic Peninsula, and mapped unknown gap between Gerlache Strait and Orleans Channel; discovered and mapped Crown Prince Gustav Channel; dog sledged to 66·05° S on the east side of the peninsula; *Antarctic* visited Tierra del Fuego, Falkland Islands, and South Georgia (visited Royal Bay and anchored in Grytviken) in the 1902 winter. At the end of that winter the ship could not reach Snow Hill Island, 3 men landed at Hope Bay to attempt to proceed overland but they failed to reach the island, so were forced to winter at Hope Bay in 1903 with minimal supplies. *Antarctic* was crushed in the pack ice of Erebus and Terror Gulf and company (20 men and the cat) wintered on Paulet Island in 1903, Ole Christian Wennersgaard died, 7 June 1903. Three search expeditions dispatched in 1903 (*Français* [1903–05], *Frithjof* [1903–04], and *Uruguay* [1903]) and a fourth was ready (*Scotia*, 1902–04); all 3 parties rescued by the Argentine naval vessel *Uruguay* (Julian Irizar), November 1903. The expedition conducted a comprehensive scientific programme including work in the Falkland Islands and Tierra del Fuego. An artist, Frank Wilbert Stokes, was aboard for the first summer.

1901–04 British National Antarctic Expedition

Robert Falcon Scott   *Discovery*

Made the first extensive exploration on land in Antarctica; spent 2 winters at Hut Point, Ross Island (45 men wintered in 1902 and 37 in 1903); a sledge party of 3 reached farthest south 82·28° S, 30 December 1902; examined the coast of Victoria Land and the Ross Ice Shelf; discovered King Edward VII Land; dogs used for hauling (cats also wintered). Ascents made in a tethered hydrogen balloon, *Eva*, 4 February 1902, reaching about 250 m (the earliest Antarctic flights, first by Scott, second by Ernest Henry Shackleton). In 1902–03 *Discovery* remained ice-bound in McMurdo Sound, where visited by Morgenen. One man died, 11 March 1902. In February 1904 Discovery was freed, after the arrival of *Morning* and *Terra Nova*; visited Macquarie Island on the outward voyage, Balleny Islands, Auckland Islands, and Falkland Islands during the return voyage. Electric lighting system used (wind powered). Comprehensive scientific programme conducted.

1902–03 British relief expedition

William Robinson Colbeck   *Morgenen* [*Morning*]

Organized by the Royal Geographical Society, carried stores and dispatches to *Discovery* in McMurdo Sound, took 8 *Discovery* men back; discovered and surveyed Scott Island (first named Markham Island), where a party landed and claimed it for Britain, 25 December 1902; landed on Possession Island; geological specimens collected on both landings. [The vessel was originally *Morgenen* but the translation to *Morning* was made for the next expedition, 1903–04.]

1902–04 Scottish National Antarctic Expedition (Britain)

William Speirs Bruce
Thomas Robertson   *Scotia*

First oceanographic exploration of Weddell Sea; discovered northern part of Caird Coast, Coats Land, but no landing possible; *Scotia*, with a complement of 33, wintered at Laurie Island, South Orkney Islands, where a meteorological observatory, 'Omond House' was established, 1 April 1903 (currently the oldest continuous one operating in the Antarctic), and the island charted; Alan Ramsay, engineer, died, 6 August 1903; his grave is the first in the island's cemetery. Further operation of meteorological station entrusted to the Oficina Meteorologica Argentina from 22 February 1904. *Scotia* visited the Falkland Islands (December 1902, December 1903, and February 1904) and Gough Island (April 1904). Conducted a comprehensive scientific programme; made ciné pictures and sound recordings; sledge dogs used for transport; prepared to search for the Swedish South Polar Expedition (1901–04) but found that Uruguay (1903) had rescued it. [Bruce subsequently planned a major expedition which, among many other objects, included a trans-Antarctic traverse. This was to begin in 1911 but did not eventuate.]

1903 South Orkney Islands; on 29 December the British Minister in Buenos Aires invited, at the request of William Speirs Bruce (Leader of the Scottish National Antarctic Expedition, 1902–04), the Argentine Government to take over and maintain the Scottish National Antarctic Expedition's meteorological observatory, established on Laurie Island on 1 April 1903. The Argentine Government accepted this and Decree 3073, of 2 January 1904, authorized the Oficina Meteorologica Argentina, of the Ministry of Agriculture, to maintain the station. Argentine personnel sailed aboard *Scotia* and the transfer took place on 22 February 1904, Robert Cockburn Mossman of the Scottish expedition remained in charge of the station until February 1905. Subsequently there has been an annual relief voyage. [One of the 3 Argentine personnel opened a Post Office there and made the first cancellations, 20 February 1904, using Falkland Islands and Argentine postage stamps (this functioned only during that month; another was established in 1941).]

1903 Argentine relief expedition

Julian Irízar   *Uruguay*

Naval vessel visited the South Shetland Islands; rescued Swedish South Polar Expedition and men of *Antarctic*, from Snow Hill Island, November; Chandler Bannen was Chilean representative aboard. [On arrival of this expedition in Buenos Aires, Carl Anton Larsen aroused interest in whaling off South Georgia, and the Compañia Argentina de Pesca was formed with Argentine capital, 29 February 1904.]

1903–04 British relief expedition

William Robinson Colbeck   *Morning*
Henry Duncan Mackay   *Terra Nova*

Organized by the Royal Navy, joined *Discovery* in McMurdo Sound to assist the return of the National Antarctic Expedition (1901–04); the 3 ships sailed north on 19 February 1904. Sighted Scott Island, visited the Auckland Islands. *Terra Nova* visited the Falkland Islands during the return voyage.

1903–04 Swedish relief expedition

Hans Olof Fredrik Gylden   *Frithjof*

Sailed to rescue the Swedish South Polar Expedition; reached Snow Hill Island to discover that wintering parties there and at Hope Bay, and the company of Antarctic, had already been rescued by *Uruguay* (Julían Irízar). Axel Alexander Klinckowstrom made ornithological observations, mainly of penguins, at Hope Bay.

1903–05 French Antarctic Expedition

Jean-Baptiste Etienne August Charcot   *Français*

Intended to search for the Swedish South Polar Expedition (1901–04) but found this had been rescued; *Français*, with a complement of 22 men, wintered at a station on Booth Island, off the west coast of the Antarctic Peninsula, 1904; charted west side of Palmer Archipelago, partly by dog sledge; discovered and roughly charted Loubet Coast southwards to Adelaide Island; sighted Hugo Island and Alexander Island; pigs and cats also aboard; undertook a comprehensive scientific programme.

1904 Norwegian and Argentine whaling enterprise

Carl Anton Larsen (Manager)
Thorvald Christian Thorsen   *Louise*
Julius Lokke   *Rolf*
Carl A. Hansen   *Fortuna* (whale-catcher)

The Compañia Argentina de Pesca, registered in Buenos Aires, established the first Antarctic whaling station on South Georgia, at Grytviken, 16 November 1904, this operated until 1965. Erik Sörling, of the Naturhistoriska Riksmuseet, Stockholm, made biological observations and collections; Larsen and Sörling began taking meteorological observations, 17 January 1905, which were maintained by Erik Nordenhaag from August, the observations have subsequently been continuous. [Larsen was accompanied by most of his family; this event was the beginning of the modern Antarctic whaling industry and permanent occupation of the island. *Louise* remained as a storage hulk until burnt in 1987. The sealers' cemetery, near Grytviken, was adopted by the whalers.]

1907–09 British Antarctic Expedition

Ernest Henry Shackleton
Rupert England (1907–08) and
Frederick Pryce Evans (1908–09)   *Nimrod*
Frederick Pryce Evans (1907)   *Koonya*

Party of 15 men wintered at Cape Royds on Ross Island; climbed Mount Erebus (3794 m), 10 March 1908; Shackleton and 3 others sledged to a farthest south of 88.38° S (01.62° [180 km] from the South Pole) when insufficient supplies necessitated their return, 9 January 1909; discovered nearly 500 km of the Transantarctic Range flanking the Ross Ice Shelf; discovered coal at Mount Buckley. Shackleton took possession of the Polar Plateau for King Edward VII, 9 January 1909; Professor Tannatt William Edgeworth David reached the region of the South Magnetic Pole and took possession for Britain of Victoria Land there, 16 January 1909, and at Cape Bernacchi, 17 October 1908. Dogs and ponies used for some sledge hauling. Visited Macquarie Island, searched for 'Dougherty's Island'. First experiments in motor transport in Antarctica, an Arrol Johnston motor car was used with limited success; ciné pictures of penguins and seals were made. The expedition used New Zealand postage stamps specially overprinted 'King Edward VII Land' and an expedition canceller; Shackleton was appointed Post-Master. Book, *Aurora Australis*, printed at Cape Royds, about 100 copies made. [To conserve coal, in January 1908, *Nimrod* was towed 2700 km from Lyttelton to the ice edge by *Koonya* (reached 66.52° S) which visited Campbell Island during the return journey.]

1908–10 French Antarctic Expedition

Jean-Baptiste Etienne August Charcot

Ernest Chollet   *Pourquoi Pas ?*

Visited the South Shetland Islands, bunkered at Deception Island, *Pourquoi Pas ?*, with a complement of 29 men, wintered at Petermann Island in 1909. Charted west coast of the Antarctic Peninsula and islands southwards to Adelaide Island and Alexander Island; discovered Marguerite Bay, Fallieres Coast, and 'Charcot Land' (later proved to be an island, Charcot Island); sighted Peter Iøy. Expedition carried 3 motor sledges but was able to use them only experimentally. Pursued a comprehensive scientific programme.

1910–12 Norwegian Antarctic Expedition

Roald Engelbregt Gravning Amundsen
Thorvald Nilsen   *Fram*

Fram reached 78·65° S; party of 9 wintered in 'Framheim' at the Bay of Whales, Ross Ice Shelf, 5 men (Amundsen, Olav Olavsen Bjaaland, Helmer Julius Hanssen, Sverre Helge Hassel, and Oscar Wisting) reached the South Pole ('Polheim'), 14 December 1911 (after adjustment for the International Date Line) by dog sledge, and claimed the South Polar Plateau for Norway ('King Haakon VII Vidde'); discovered Queen Maud Mountains. Kristian Prestrud explored King Edward VII Land and took possession for King Haakon, 7 December 1911; reported 'Carmen Land', the existence of which has been disproved. During the 1911 winter *Fram* investigated non-existent 'Nimrod Island' and 'Dougherty's Island', and made oceanographic observations in the South Atlantic. Ciné pictures of some activities were produced.

1910–12 Japanese Antarctic expedition

Nobu Shirase
Naokichi Nomura   *Kainan Maru*

Sailed from Tokyo Bay with a complement of 27; reached Coulman Island, Ross Sea, in 1910–11 but failed to penetrate the pack ice and wintered in Sydney, Australia. During 1911–12 reached the edge of the Ross Ice Shelf and landed at the Bay of Whales, from where a party sledged (with Ainu dog handlers) some distance south-east, a 'Dash Patrol' was made 250 km inland which claimed the area within sight, 'Yamato Yukihara' ('Yamato Snow Plain'), on the Ross Ice Shelf, for Japan, 28 January 1912. Separate party landed on King Edward VII Land. Ciné pictures were produced.

1910–13 British Antarctic Expedition

Robert Falcon Scott
Henry Lewin Lee Pennell   *Terra Nova*

Spent 2 winters (25 men in 1911, 13 men in 1912) at Cape Evans on Ross Island; 5 men (Scott, Henry Robertson Bowers, Edgar Evans, Lawrence Edward Grace Oates, and Edward Adrian Wilson) reached the South Pole, 17 January 1912 by man-hauling, and found Amundsen's expedition had departed there 33 days previously; all perished during the return journey. Extensive exploration and scientific investigations conducted (biology, geology, glaciology, meteorology, geophysics) along the coast of Victoria Land and on the Ross Ice Shelf. Separate party of 6 men (led by Victor Lindsay Arbuthnot Campbell) wintered at Cape Adare (1911) and Evans Cove (1912); discovered Oates Land. Herbert George Ponting, present for the first winter, made first moving picture documentary film of an Antarctic expedition, *90° South* (previous expeditionary cinematography was only of brief excerpts), prepared colour photographs; expedition deployed a telephone, Cape Evans to Hut Point; established a Post Office using New Zealand postage stamps overprinted 'Victoria Land' and an expedition canceller. Ponies, mules, 'motorised sledges', and dogs were used for transport in addition to man-hauling.

1911–12 German South Polar Expedition

Wilhelm Filchner
Richard Vahsel (1911–12) and
Alfred Kling (1912)   *Deutschland*

Visited South Georgia and South Sandwich Islands; at the former investigated the coasts aboard *Undine*, prepared charts and re-opened the observatory at Royal Bay. Continued south to 'Prinzregent Luitpold Land' [Luitpold Coast] and charted part of the south coast of the Weddell Sea; discovered the Filchner Ice Shelf where an attempt to establish a station was unsuccessful. *Deutschland*, with 33 men aboard, was beset and drifted in pack ice for 9 months; a winter sledge journey proved non-existence of Robert Johnson's 'New South Greenland', described in 1821. Visited South Georgia a second time after getting free of the ice. Sledge dogs and Manchurian ponies carried for transport. [Vahsel died, 8 August 1912; succeeded by Kling. The expedition originally intended to cross Antarctica.]

1911–14 Australasian Antarctic Expedition

Douglas Mawson (Leader)
John King Davis   *Aurora*
Thomas Holyman   *Toroa* (1911)

Discovered and explored King George V Land and

Queen Mary Land, which were claimed for the British Crown at Cape Denison, March 1912, and at Possession Rocks, 25 December 1912; shore parties wintered at Cape Denison (18 men in 1912 and 7 in 1913) and on the Shackleton Ice Shelf (leader John Robert Francis [Frank] Wild, 8 men); the former explored Terre Adélie and sledged to the South Magnetic Pole, which was determined by Eric Norman Webb, 21 December 1912, and more territory was claimed; the latter reached Gaussberg on 23 December 1912 and left a message; both undertook extensive scientific programmes, dogs used for hauling (received from Roald Amundsen aboard *Fram*). The Cape Denison station was manned for 1913 winter to await the return of a 3 man sledging party led by Mawson (Mawson alone returned, on the day after the ship departed). A separate party, of 5 men, led by George F. Ainsworth, spent 23 months on Macquarie Island, made the first detailed scientific investigations there, mapped the island, and introduced sheep. Wireless stations were established at Cape Denison and Macquarie Island (as a relay); first radio contact with Australia made 4 January 1912 and with Antarctica on 25 September 1912; sheep, dogs, and hens introduced, vegetables planted. Intended to take an aircraft to Antarctica, but it crashed in Australia during the outward voyage and was used without wings as an 'air tractor sledge'. Colour and ciné photographs produced by several members of the expedition. Traces of silver, gold, and cassiterite were detected, and a meteorite was found. *Aurora* searched for the non-existent 'Royal Company Island' (31 May to 2 June 1912) and visited Auckland Islands, 24 June to 6 July 1912 (reported no trace of the Enderby Settlement at Hardwicke). [*Toroa* was chartered to convey stores and personnel to Macquarie Island in 1911, and *Tutanekai* in 1913.]

1913–15 Commonwealth Meteorological Expedition (Australia)

Harold Power (1914) and A. C. Tulloch (1915)
(leaders of winter parties)
George William Charles Bedford   *Endeavour*
Meteorological station established on Macquarie Island by the Australasian Antarctic Expedition transferred to the Commonwealth Meteorological Service. *Endeavour*, with a full complement aboard, disappeared without trace after relieving the station on 3 December 1914 (probably foundered on Macquarie Island). Breeding sheep (28), poultry, and ducks were introduced and an attempt made to start a pastoral

industry. The station was maintained until 4 December 1915, when it was closed owing to the difficulty of securing a vessel for annual relief during the First World War; men taken off by *Rachel Cohen* (W. J. MacBryde).

1914–16 Imperial Trans-Antarctic Expedition [Weddell Sea Party] (Britain)

Sir Ernest Henry Shackleton
Frank Arthur Worsley   *Endurance*
Visited South Georgia and South Sandwich Islands; discovered southern part of Caird Coast. *Endurance*, with a complement of 28 men, was beset, drifted 10 months during which the non-existence of Robert Johnson's 'New South Greenland' was demonstrated; *Endurance* was crushed in pack ice of the Weddell Sea, and sunk on 27 October 1915, wrecking the plan to sledge across Antarctica; company drifted on the pack ice where wintered and later escaped in boats to Elephant Island, South Shetland Islands, 14 April 1916; Shackleton with 5 others sailed 1450 km to South Georgia in modified whale boat *James Caird*; he and 2 of them made the first major trek across the island to Stromness; 5 relief expeditions were organized in 1916, of which the fourth rescued the party from Elephant Island which was led by John Robert Francis [Frank] Wild after Shackleton's departure. [*Endurance* was equipped with wireless telegraphy apparatus but it was insufficiently powerful to reach a coast station; dogs used for sledge hauling and a motor sledge carried; James Francis [Frank] Hurley made a ciné film and took colour photographs.]

1914–17 Imperial Trans-Antarctic Expedition [Ross Sea Party] (Britain)

Æneas Lionel Acton Mackintosh (1914–15) and
Joseph Russell Stenhouse (1915–16)   *Aurora*
Organized by Sir Ernest Henry Shackleton to meet the *Endurance* party intending to sledge from the Weddell Sea; visited Macquarie Island to provision Commonwealth Meteorological Expedition there, December 1914; continued to Cape Evans, Ross Island, where it was intended the vessel remain for winter. On 6 May 1915 *Aurora* was driven from the moorings by a blizzard, leaving 10 men ashore who wintered at Cape Evans with minimal supplies and laid depots southwards towards the Beardmore Glacier for Shackleton's proposed trans-Antarctic expedition, dogs used for hauling and a motor sledge carried. *Aurora* became beset, then drifted for 10 months in Ross Sea pack ice

passing the Balleny Islands, until freed on 14 March 1916, and reached New Zealand. The 7 survivors of the shore party were rescued, 10 January 1917. [Mackintosh commanded *Aurora* during the outward voyage and remained ashore from January 1915, he died crossing sea ice, 8 May 1916; Stenhouse took command of the ship on 10 May 1915. Expedition had wireless telegraphy apparatus, contact was made with Cape Evans from *Aurora*, and signals were received from Macquarie Island, it was insufficiently powerful to reach a coast station.]

1916 British [first] relief expedition (from South Georgia)

Sir Ernest Henry Shackleton

Ingvar O. Thom   *Southern Sky*

Failed to reach Elephant Island, South Shetland Islands, May, to rescue Shackleton's party left there, April 1916; conveyed Shackleton to the Falkland Islands.

1916 Uruguayan [second] relief expedition (from Montevideo)

Sir Ernest Henry Shackleton

Ruperto L. Elichiribehety   *Instituto de Pesca No I*

Called at the Falkland Islands where took Shackleton aboard; failed to reach Elephant Island, South Shetland Islands, June, to rescue Shackleton's party left there, April 1916.

1916 British [third] relief expedition (from Punta Arenas)

Sir Ernest Henry Shackleton   *Emma*

Chartered vessel failed to reach Elephant Island, July, to rescue Shackleton's party left there, April 1916. Escorted for part of voyage by *Yelcho*.

1916 Chilean [fourth] relief expedition (from Punta Arenas)

Sir Ernest Henry Shackleton

Luis Alberto Pardo Villalon   *Yelcho*

Rescued men of *Endurance* from Elephant Island, 30 August. [*Discovery* (James Fairweather) sailed from Plymouth to assist in the rescue (fifth relief expedition); reached Montevideo where heard of *Yelcho*'s success.]

1916–17 British relief expedition (from Port Chalmers)

John King Davis   *Aurora*

After extensive refitting in New Zealand, *Aurora*

rescued the 7 survivors of the Ross Sea party of the Imperial Trans-Antarctic Expedition Ross Sea party from Ross Island, 10 January 1917 (3 men had perished). Sir Ernest Henry Shackleton accompanied the voyage.

1920–22 British Expedition to Graham Land

John Lachlan Cope

Four men were taken to the South Shetland Islands by whaling vessels; they intended to sledge southwards from Hope Bay but ice conditions prevented access; the leader and George Hubert Wilkins returned to Britain, but in 1921 Thomas Wyatt Bagshawe and Maxime Charles Lester wintered at Waterboat Point on the west coast of the Antarctic Peninsula, recording meteorological (complete year of data obtained), tidal and zoological observations until relieved, 13 January 1922, by the whaling vessel Svend Foyn (Ole Andersen), with Arthur George Bennett, Falkland Islands Dependencies Administrator, aboard. [This expedition was planned as a far more comprehensive operation but was unable to obtain sufficient finance.]

1921–22 Shackleton-Rowett Antarctic Expedition (Britain)

Sir Ernest Henry Shackleton and

John Robert Francis [Frank] Wild   *Quest*

Visited South Georgia, where Shackleton died, 5 January 1922. Wild took command and expedition continued to the Weddell Sea; visited the South Sandwich Islands; confirmed non-existence of 'New South Greenland'; attempts to discover new land in the Enderby Land region were unsuccessful; visited Elephant Island, South Shetland Islands; returned to South Georgia, then visited Gough Island and Tristan da Cunha. A Post Office operated aboard *Quest*.

Shackleton at South Georgia

Robert Burton

Gateway to the Antarctic

'South Georgia must ever be to us who were Shackleton's men the home of many memories. Its whalers were not only ready to lend a helping hand at the Outset of the Expedition, but as will be seen later, when disaster and calamity overtook us in the Far South they came hurrying to our relief.' Frank Hurley.[1]

The island of South Georgia is a special place. For Captain Cook, it was barren and dreary, but he was no romantic. Others have written lyrically of the splendours of its wildlife and scenery ('It might have been the Himalayas seen from Simla if only one substituted cloud for the sea').[2] Many visitors to South Georgia, now numbering several thousand a year arriving on cruise ships, say that it outshines the Antarctic for spectacle and interest. However, it has one ingredient that is unique. In the words of Duncan Carse who made the first surveys of the island's interior: 'South Georgia will be remembered as journey's end for a great British polar explorer, Sir Ernest Shackleton; and that alone is enough to ensure it of a place in history'.[3] In fact, it was the end of two journeys. South Georgia was the destination of Shackleton's epic voyage from Elephant Island in the *James Caird* and it was also the end of his life's journey. The co-incidence of the hero lying buried near the scene of his triumph adds a special lustre to the history of South Georgia.

Shackleton visited South Georgia three times. His first visit was on *Endurance*, prior to disappearing into the Weddell Sea, which formed a foundation for the subsequent visits: the drama of the 'Great Antarctic Rescue' and his death and burial eight years later. So mundane was the first visit that accounts of the month-long stay are omitted from *South*, Shackleton's own account of the expedition, and also from Frank Worsley's book *Endurance*. Nevertheless, Shackleton had recognised South Georgia's importance by calling it 'The Gateway to the Antarctic'. The island had been the springboard for earlier expeditions into the Weddell Sea but Shackleton only decided to call there when *Endurance* reached Buenos Aires. The original plan had been to visit Port Stanley in the Falkland Islands but Shackleton was apparently put off by reports of

German warships in the area. A call at South Georgia would also enable him to complete his stores at the whaling stations, and the island was 1,500 kilometres closer to his destination on the coastline of Antarctica.

On November 5, 1914, the watch on *Endurance* glimpsed land through falling snow but could make out little because the mountain tops were hidden by low cloud. Frank Hurley claimed that they were able literally to navigate by their noses because of the increasingly strong smell of rotting flesh from the whaling stations. They found themselves being followed by three whalecatchers and, closing with the *Sitka*, they accepted an offer to pilot them into King Edward Cove. There they anchored off Grytviken, the whaling station of the Compañia Argentina de Pesca established by Captain C. A. Larsen eleven years earlier.

Discussions with the Norwegian whalers soon led Shackleton again to modify his programme, because they reported the worst ice ever recorded and recommended that he wait for it to disperse. Instead of spending no more than a few days collecting stores, he remained at South Georgia for a month. These were halcyon days, a quiet interval before the adventures that awaited *Endurance* in the Weddell Sea. Shackleton begins his narrative in *South* only on December 5, the day that they sailed from South Georgia, and the expedition's activities at South Georgia have to be pieced together from diaries and letters.

Shackleton was busy persuading station managers to part with stores against 'notes of hand'. One of these still exists in the form of a brief letter requesting three drums of paraffin from Captain Søren Berntsen, the manager of Husvik whaling station. Shackleton does not seem to have arranged any organised Antarctic training except that the motor sledges were tried out while a little snow remained and the dogs were taken ashore and tethered by the cemetery. Their six handlers moved into the small hospital near the cemetery and held training sessions with their charges on the ice-covered Gull Lake on the plateau above. They also dug out a bathing pool in the snow-fed stream that ran past the hospital. Macklin would lie down in the icy water and then stand in the snow to dry himself.

To Captain Thom with kindest regards from Ernest Shackleton. Nov 1914

Norwegian whalers are welcomed on board *Endurance* at anchor in South Georgia, in November 1914. Shackleton (1st. left) and Worsley (2nd. from right) are in uniform. The Norwegians include some who were involved in the rescue from Elephant Island. They are Søren Berntsen (4th from left, in front) of Husvik, Ingvar Thom (5th from left, at back), who skippered *Southern Sky* in the first attempted relief of Elephant Island, Leganger Hansen (4th from right) of Leith Harbour, and Thoralf Sørlle (first right) of Stromness. (Karl Jan Skontorp)

On his own initiative, the physicist Reginald James, aided by Hubert Hudson, the navigation officer, set up two red and white striped posts aligned north-south, called meridian transit beacons, to enable the skippers of whalecatchers to swing their compasses. Clark, the biologist, made collecting trips and wrote a report on the unpleasant conditions at the whaling stations, emphasising the great waste through abandoning the carcasses after the blubber had been stripped. As a result regulations were brought in to ensure that every part of the whale was used.

Hurley missed no opportunity to make expeditions in search of new subjects. He arranged for outings on whalecatchers and traversed the coast in the antiquated sealer *Lille Carl*, famous for having once taken the Kaiser on a whaling expedition in Norway but now: 'perilously thin and rusty in her plates, leaky of boiler and asthmatic in her tubes'.[4]

Socialising with the whalers included dinners at the 'Villa', as the houses of the station managers were known. These superior officials of the whaling companies lived in style. Shackleton wrote that their homes were like an advertisement for a modern hotel 'replete with every comfort'.[5] The Grytviken Villa 'boasted a billiard table, piano and a charming collection of geraniums blooming in the bow-windows'.[6] There were also more riotous evenings with the whaling employees, such as the 'gramophone fling' with the Scots employed by Salvesen at Leith Harbour. With the aid of gramophone records of bagpipe music and a few bottles of whisky, the guests were treated to displays of reels, jigs and hornpipes. Hurley wrote that 'it was a great exhibition of endurance in which we all shared in different ways'.[7]

Finally, 'an Entertainment' was held aboard *Endurance* in honour of the Norwegians who had given generous and unstinting assistance. Then, on their last night at South Georgia, the ship's company was invited

Frank Hurley, A panorama of King Edward Cove and the surrounding country, showing Mount Hodges. It illustrates the rugged, but grand, nature of the terrain that makes overland travel so difficult. *Endurance* is at anchor, and the Grytviken whaling station is at the head of the cove. (Royal Geographical Society Picture Library)

to the Grytviken Villa by the manager Fridthjof Jacob-sen. Some of them decided to play a practical joke on Hubert Hudson, a humourless character who, as result, was always having his leg pulled. He was told that it was to be a fancy dress party and decided to go as a buddha, clad in nothing but a sheet and with a kettle-lid tied on his head. It was snowing heavily as he was rowed ashore alone and he was half-frozen when he arrived, to great acclamation, at the 'Villa'. Thereafter, he was known as 'Buddha'.[8]

The time spent at South Georgia would pay an unex-pected dividend. By cruising to and fro along the coast Shackleton and Worsley gained firsthand knowledge of the geography of the island which would guide their crossing of its unmapped hinterland sixteen months later.

Exit from the Antarctic
The sun had disappeared behind the hills when Shack-leton, Worsley and Crean crossed the flat ground

behind the whaling station at Stromness on May 19, 1916. We can imagine them stumbling over the last few hundred metres in a combination of utter exhaustion and sheer elation as they approached Journey's End. If South Georgia was the 'Gateway to the Antarctic', it was also the 'Emergency Exit'. In a letter to his friend, Harold Begbie, Shackleton wrote that 'when we got to the whaling station, it was the thought of those com-rades that made us so mad with joy. We didn't so much feel that we were safe as that they would be saved'.[9]

When reading their own accounts of the journey from Elephant Island, it is easy to forget the men's state of mind and body. Little is made of their mental and physical plight; instead they recall details that had no place in the grim battle for survival. After all their toils and tribulations, Worsley suddenly worries about his state of dress because 'there might be women here'. He produces three large safety pins to effect essential repairs to his clothes and refuses to let Shackleton have one. But, as Shackleton says, he only drew attention to his own deficiencies.[10]

Their appearance was certainly outlandish and it is not surprising that two young men turned and ran at the trio's approach. Matthias Andersen, the station foreman, recalled forty years later how he was directing the unloading of a ship when he heard a shout and saw them running as fast as their legs could carry them. Behind them three figures were slowly approaching. He was puzzled because they were not dressed like seamen but wore ragged anoraks and their faces were black and bearded.

'Can you take us to Captain Andersen?', asked one man in English.

'My name is Andersen', replied Andersen.

'No, Anton Andersen'.

Mathias Andersen then explained that Anton Andersen was no longer station manager at Stromness and had been replaced by Thoralf Sørlle.

'Are there any ships sailing to England?'

'No', Andersen answered as he led them to the 'Villa', the manager's house.[11]

Accounts of the meeting with Sørlle, as with other details in this part of the *Endurance* story, differ. It is difficult to know who had the most accurate memory or whether someone is embroidering a good story. Worsley has been cited as the epitome of accuracy. There is, of course, no doubt that his navigation of the *James Caird* was phenomenal, but he is known not to have let the truth stand in the way of a good story. The true course of events has also been distorted by later authors adding their own embellishments.

Worsley wrote that Andersen left them outside while he went in and told Sørlle, 'There are three funny-looking men outside; they say they know you'.[12] Sørlle went to the door in his shirt sleeves and looked horrified at the men on the doorstep.

'Who the hell are you?' he asked, according to Andersen. Not an overwhelming welcome but understandable.[13]

Once Shackleton had identified himself, after Sørlle had doubtfully suggested that he might be the mate of the *Daisy* (the last American open-boat whaling vessel, which had visited South Georgia in 1913), suspicion gave way to boundless hospitality. We can speculate how much the extra special treatment received by Shackleton and his men was due to the month that *Endurance* had spent at South Georgia, when whalers and explorers had got to know each other.

'Come in, come in!', said Sørlle, almost dragging Shackleton and his companions indoors, barely giving them time to remove their boots and shrugging off protests about their smell.

'That doesn't matter, we're used to it on a whaling-station!'[14]

This is a more believable reaction to Shackleton's unexpected appearance than the story that Sørlle and other Norwegians shed a tear. This was said to have been witnessed by a whaler who was still working at South Georgia in the 1950s, but no such man existed.

Worsley says that Shackleton asked Sørlle to take a photograph of them but had no film, and 'the world lost a picture of its three dirtiest men'. It seems that another camera was found and this photograph was taken some time later. Unfortunately the provenance of this photograph is not known, but it was presumably taken after Worsley's return from King Haakon Bay. The pale skin on the lower half of Shackleton's face shows that his beard has recently been removed. He is wearing the hat in which he appears in photographs taken later in Port Stanley and Punta Arenas. The men's faces show the strain of their experience, although Worsley's face is partly obscured by a woollen helmet or anorak hood.

The Villa was always an oasis of comfort amid the squalor of a whaling station, and soon the trio was seated in armchairs with coffee, bread and jam, scones and cakes – the first civilised meal since leaving the sinking *Endurance* six months earlier and a welcome change from meat, blubber and hardtack biscuit – and learning the horrors of the First World War. I cannot think of any other subject that would have prevented them nodding off as they relaxed in the warmth and comfort of Sørlle's parlour. Meanwhile, the steward, who 'looked after us like a hen with three chicks, and evidently considered us as his own peculiar property', in Worsley's words, ran a bath and collected new sets of clothes from the station's 'slop chest'.[15] Imagine the pleasure of discarding their awful garments and subsiding into a hot bath to ease aching limbs and soak away the accumulated filth! A shave restored them to civilised appearance and the new suits completed the transformation.

By the time they had had dinner with Captain Sørlle, steam had been raised in the whalecatcher *Samson*, and Worsley went on board to guide the rescue of Macnish, McCarthy and Vincent from Peggotty Bluff on the other side of the island. Worsley retired to his bunk and slept through the rising storm that would have spelled certain death if it had arrived at South Georgia a day earlier. When he awoke after eleven hours' sleep, *Samson* was entering King Haakon Bay. A blast of the

Tom Crean, Sir Ernest Shackleton and Frank Worsley photographed soon after their arrival at Stromness, when their faces still show the effects of their ordeal. Close examination of the print shows the lower half of Shackleton's face is pale, indicating his beard has been removed no more than a few days earlier. The identification of the man on the right as Worsley has been disputed, but his face is partly obscured by a woollen helmet. (Hon. Alexandra Shackleton. Scott Polar Research Institute)

steam whistle brought the three tumbling out of the *James Caird* and they were soon aboard and heading back to Stromness. In fact, the storm drove them to seek shelter at Grytviken and they eventually put into Leith Harbour in the evening of the 21st, bringing the *James Caird* and her equipment with them.

Meanwhile, the magistrate, Edward Binnie, had come round from Grytviken to see what assistance he could render, but arrangements for rescuing the men on Elephant Island were already in hand. Sørlle had taken Shackleton and Crean round to Husvik whaling station, where Søren Berntsen, the manager gave Shackleton the same open-handed welcome as Sørlle had on the previous day. The whalecatcher *Southern Sky*, belonging to the British Southern Sealing and Whaling Company, was laid up for the winter, and work was immediately put in hand to prepare her for sea. The problem of arranging the charter was solved by

Shackleton accepting responsibility for the ship, although both parties must have known that there was little security to support this. There was no shortage of volunteers to crew *Southern Sky*, and Shackleton asked Ingvar Thom, captain of the *Orwell*, a transport ship lying at Husvik, to serve as skipper. Probably nothing better reveals the esteem in which Shackleton was held at South Georgia than the willingness of the Norwegians to help his expedition out of its dire straits and organise their rescue so quickly.

One of Binnie's duties as a magistrate was to hold an enquiry into the loss of *Endurance* but he, in consultation with Shackleton and the whaling managers, decided that the priority was to get *Southern Sky* to sea and hold the enquiry when she returned with the crew. That, as we know, never happened and they eventually landed at Punta Arenas. Rather oddly, the Governor of the Falkland Islands sent Binnie a letter, long after

Shackleton had arrived in Port Stanley, asking whether an enquiry had been held.

With *Samson*'s return and the party reunited, they were entertained at Husvik by the Norwegian whaling skippers and mates, with 'faces lined and seamed by the storms of half a century'. Worsley wrote that they gathered in a big club-room, but Shackleton in *South* describes the meeting as being held on the *Orwell*. This is a strange discrepancy to find in the recollection of an occasion that made a great impression on both men. There was no club-room as such as Husvik and the meeting was probably held in one of the barracks, called 'Orwell-brakka' in Norwegian. Nevertheless, Shackleton and Worsley agreed about the reception they received from the Norwegian seamen. A 'white-haired veteran of the sea' made a short speech translated by Berntsen. Worsley describes the scene: the old whaler said 'that never had he heard of such a wonderful feat of daring seamanship as bringing the 22-foot open boat from Elephant Island to South Georgia, and then to crown it, tramping across the snow and rocky heights of the interior, and that he felt it an honour to meet and shake hands with Sir Ernest and his comrades. He finished with a dramatic gesture:

'These are men'.

All the seamen present then came forward and solemnly shook hands with us in turn. Coming from brother seamen, men of our own class and members of a great seafaring race like the Norwegians, this was a wonderful tribute and one of which we all felt proud.'[16]

The three men had every reason to be proud of their achievement, but the strain had told. A revealing glimpse into their mental state is given by Søren Berntsen in a letter to his wife in which he relates how he heard them 'make an awful noise in their sleep – they thought that they were back at sea in the small boat'.[17]

Refitting *Southern Sky* was soon completed, and at 9 a.m. on 23rd. May, she steamed out of Husvik, bound for Elephant Island, and with every hope of being back in ten days. But this was not to be. Pack ice held her up and she returned to Port Stanley where Shackleton could use the telegraph to contact the outside world and arrange another rescue bid. In the event, it took three more attempts before the twenty-two men marooned on Elephant Island were brought to safety by the Chilean tug *Yelcho*.

The Last Expedition
On 4 January 1922, the Shackleton-Rowett expedition reached South Georgia on the converted sealer *Quest*.

For Shackleton and Worsley it was a return to the scene of their desperate but triumphant crossing of the island. They excitedly pointed out to everyone the route that they had taken out of the mountains. Several of the men noted in their diaries that Shackleton, who had been rather low during the voyage south and increasingly weary as they approached South Georgia, was in high spirits and much more like the 'Boss' of old.

This was the expedition that should not have been: an ill-found ship, no grand plan and an ailing leader. Yet it provided a fitting end to a heroic story, with the valiant leader gathering his band of loyal followers and returning to his scene of triumph to die. If Shackleton had died at any other place, it would have been simply a great loss, but his sudden death at South Georgia created a dramatic finale to the saga of the *Endurance*. He is buried on a remote, wild and beautiful island which has enough trappings of civilisation to provide a simple cemetery in a grand setting. His grave has become a place of pilgrimage where hundreds of visitors gather every year to toast 'The Boss'.

For seven of the crew who had sailed on *Endurance*, *Quest*'s landfall was the first they had seen of South Georgia, its magnificent scenery and stinking whaling stations, since they had left for the Weddell Sea eight years earlier. Once anchored in the familiar spot in King Edward Cove, they could relax from nursing the *Quest* through stormy seas. Hussey wrote that Shackleton was full of jokes that evening and announced as they retired that they would celebrate Christmas next day. Christmas Day had been spent riding out a gale and their fare had been corned beef sandwiches. Now they could enjoy the tinned ham and turkey and plum puddings donated by Mr. and Mrs. Rowett.

Hussey continued: 'shortly before three a.m. during the night I was wakened by Macklin, saying: 'Wake up, Huss, get a hypodermic and come at once to the Boss. He is dying!' It was a terrible shock, but I jumped out of my bunk at once and took certain medicines to Shackleton's cabin. But already it was too late. Nothing could be done. I noted the time – it was about two-fifty a.m'.[18]

Macklin made notes on Shackleton's last minutes an hour after the event. He had been on anchor watch when he heard the whistle in Shackleton's cabin and found him sitting up in bed.

'Hullo, Mack, boy, is that you? I thought it was. I can't sleep to-night, can you get me a sleeping draught?'

He allowed Macklin to fuss around him, making up the medicine, fetching a blanket and tucking him up. Macklin decided this was a good moment for some

Sir Ernest Shackleton's coffin is carried from the Whalers' Church, Grytviken. It is preceded by Leonard Hussey, in white yachting cap, and the magistrate, Edward Binnie. (Edward Binnie Collection. © Thomas Binnie Jr.)

words of advice, telling him that he had to take things easy and that a single dose of medicine was not the answer.

'You are always wanting me to give up something. What do you want me to give up now?'

'Chiefly alcohol, Boss. I don't think it agrees with you.'

He then said 'I can feel the pain coming on again. Give me the medicine quickly.'

Those were his last words as he suffered his fatal heart attack.[19]

Macklin ran to call McIlroy and Hussey but they could do nothing. It was hard to accept. Wild remembers that he was woken with the news and repeated dully:

'The Boss dead! Dead, do you mean? He can't be dead!'[20] Hussey again: 'During the rest of that night I sat numb, a flood of memories surging through my mind. All the little incidents that make you love a man came back to me. We had passed through so many of the most adventurous times of my life together that there were bonds, indestructible bonds, uniting us. I knew then that I should never look upon his like again'.[21]

Worsley was woken, and next morning the news was

broken to the *Quest*'s company. Christopher Naisbitt, the ship's clerk, wrote, 'I had known this man for only a matter of weeks, but somehow he had made me feel to be one of his flock and with his loss I felt the bottom had fallen out of the great adventure'.[22]

Macklin knew that Shackleton had been in bad health, although he had tried to pass off an earlier heart attack as a fainting fit. Following the post mortem, Macklin wrote that what was remarkable 'is that in such an advanced condition he was able to carry on as he did. It shows, psychologically, a wonderful will power and an unyielding determination'.[23]

Frank Wild now took command of the expedition. His first action was to arrange for the news to be conveyed to Lady Shackleton. *Quest* had wireless apparatus but despite all the care of the operator, it broke down before a message could be sent. None of the whaling stations had sets but *Albuera*, a steamer lying at Leith Harbour, was due to sail in a few days, and arrangements were made to send a message as soon as it got within range of any wireless station. Meanwhile Wild organised Shackleton's body to be carried to Montevideo on a floating factory, *Professor Gruvel*. Hussey asked to accompany it as he had no heart left for the expedition and wanted to press on with his medical studies. At Montevideo, he learned of Lady Shackleton's wish for her husband to be buried at South Georgia and he returned with the body on a British ship, the *Woodville*. By this time, *Quest* and her crew had left for the Antarctic and Hussey was the only member of the expedition at Shackleton's funeral.[24]

The funeral was held on March 5th. About a hundred men gathered at the Whalers' Church, with Mrs Aarberg, the wife of the doctor at Leith Harbour. She was the only woman then living on the island and she placed on the coffin a bunch of freshly-gathered flowers from her conservatory. With no clergyman present, the magistrate, Edward Binnie, officiated at the simple service. The Norwegians sang the first verse of their funeral hymn, Binnie read part of the Burial Service, the Lord's Prayer was recited, and the second verse of the hymn was sung.

Then the coffin was carried in procession by six Shetlanders, preceded by two men carrying black funeral banners in the Norwegian custom, and with the church bell tolling. At the cemetery outside the whaling station, where British flags flew at half-mast, the final verse of the Norwegian hymn was sung, the remainder of the Burial Service read and the Lord's Prayer repeated. The grave was filled in and marked with a rough wooden cross hung with wreaths brought from Montevideo.[25] The present headstone of Scottish granite was brought down in 1928 and unveiled by the Governor of the Falkland Islands, Sir Arnold Hodson.[26]

On April 6th, *Quest* returned to South Georgia and the crew learned that Shackleton had been laid to rest there. Before they left the island a month later, they visited Grytviken and built a cairn surmounted by a cross on Hope Point, where it would be the first object seen on approaching King Edward Cove and the last

The burial in Grytviken cemetery.
The third of three photographs taken with Edward Binnie's camera, this shows wreaths being laid. Mrs. Aarberg is standing in front of the crowd, wearing a cloche hat. (Edward Binnie Collection. © Thomas Binnie Jr.)

seen on departure. Under the direction of James Dell, the bosun, every man contributed to the manufacture of the cross.

The final rite was a visit to Shackleton's grave by the old Endurances – Wild, Worsley, Macklin, McIlroy, Kerr, Green and McLeod – to pay their last respects. Worsley later wrote that, as they looked across the bay to the cairn and cross that they had just erected, he meditated on Shackleton's great deeds:

'It seemed to me that among all his achievements and triumphs, great as they were, his one failure was the most glorious. By self-sacrifice and throwing his own life into the balance he saved every one of his men – not a life was lost – although at times it had looked unlikely that one could be saved.

His outstanding characteristics were his care of, and anxiety for the lives and well-being of all his men'.[27]

Notes

1   Frank Hurley, *Argonauts of the South*, 1925, p. 139.
2   Stanley Kemp, in Alister Hardy, *Great Waters*, 1967, p. 158.
3   Duncan Carse, 'The South Georgia Survey', *The Times*, 30 July, 1954.
4   Hurley, p. 136.
5   Ernest Shackleton, Diary. Transcript in Fisher Papers, Scott Polar Research Institute.
6   Hurley, p. 133.
7   Ibid., p. 135.
8   L. D. A. Hussey, *South with Shackleton*, 1949, p. 131.
9   Quoted, ibid., p. 131.
10   Ernest Shackleton, *South*, 1919, p. 206.
11   Elvind Otto Hjelle, *Tre men kom vaklende fra isødet*. (Three Men stagger in from the icy wastes), *Billed Journalen*, 3, 1959.
12   Frank Worsley, *Shackleton's Boat Journey*,(Folio Society) 1974, p. 140.
13   See n. 11.
14   Worsley, p. 140.
15   Ibid., p. 141.
16   Ibid., p. 143.
17   James Meiklejohn and Karl Jan Skontorp, 1993, 'A resolution to the Shackleton Valley controversy', *Polar Record,* 29, p. 165.
18   Hussey, p. 171
19   Alexander Macklin, Diary. Transcript in Fisher Papers, Scott Polar Research Institute.
20   Frank Wild, *Shackleton's Last Voyage*, 1923, p. 65.
21   Hussey, p. 171.
22   Christopher Naisbitt. Transcript of conversation. Fisher Papers, Scott Polar Research Institute.
23   Macklin, Diary. Transcript in Fisher Papers, Scott Polar Research Institute.
24   Wild, p. 173.
25   L. Hussey, 'Shackleton's Burial', *The Times*, 4 May, 1922.
26   Arnold Hodson, 'Notes on a visit to the Dependencies of the Falkland Islands'. 1929. *Geographical Journal*, 73, pp. 61–63.
27   Worsley, p. 146.

The granite headstone is unveiled by the Governor of the Falkland Islands, Sir Arnold Hodson. To the left stands Mrs. Aarberg with the officers, scientists and crew of the R. R. S. *William Scoresby*. To the right are the magistrate, F. B. Allison, and the whaling managers. Thøralf Sorlle is third from the right. The photograph does not show about 80 whalers outside the cemetery. (Courtesy of Mrs. Anne Fraser)

Tom Crean, captured by the renowned photographer, Herbert Ponting, on Scott's last expedition – ready, alert and optimistic

Tom Crean: Unsung Hero

Michael Smith

Few men graced the Heroic Age of Polar exploration at the start of the twentieth century more nobly than Tom Crean. The big, smiling Irishman was a colossal figure in an era which produced a succession of great figures and outstanding tales of endurance and survival against the odds. Tom Crean was an integral part of the era, a man whose career spanned three of the four major British expeditions to the Antarctic in the opening two decades of the century. He was one of the very few people to serve both Scott and Shackleton – and he outlived them both. He first distinguished himself on the *Discovery* expedition in 1901–04 and figured more prominently on Scott's last expedition between 1910–13. But his most celebrated feats were performed on Sir Ernest Shackleton's memorable *Endurance* expedition of 1914–16.

It was on *Endurance* – officially known as the Imperial Trans-Antarctic Expedition – that Crean proved to be an invaluable and loyal lieutenant to Shackleton. He became one of the key figures in the prolonged fight for survival and played a central role in all the major events of the expedition: the fraught passage of the three lifeboats through the ice floes to Elephant Island after the *Endurance* was crushed; the courageous 800 mile open boat journey to South Georgia in the *James Caird*; the forced march across the previously unexplored mountains and glaciers of South Georgia. Shackleton had recruited Crean to *Endurance* in early 1914, only a matter of months after Crean's return from Scott's ill-fated last expedition. He was appointed Second Officer and selected for the six-man party which was scheduled to make the first-ever crossing of the Antarctic Continent, a distance of over 1,800 miles. Shackleton had known Crean from the year they spent together on *Discovery*, which in 1901 was the largest British expedition ever sent to explore the then unknown continent of Antarctica. He had also received glowing testimonials about the Irishman from members of Scott's expedition, including Lieutenant Teddy Evans whose life Crean had saved in heroic circumstances in 1912.

Shackleton, who was a master of man-management,

was attracted by Tom Crean's great reliability and formidable physical strength. In addition, he was blessed with a powerful mental strength and inner self-belief which together told Shackleton that Crean was a man who would not buckle under either the physical or psychological strain. Tom Crean was a man for tight spots and as near to being indestructible as any human could be. It was a wise choice, and during the expedition's darkest moments, when the 28 men were adrift on an ice-floe thousands of miles from safety, Shackleton came to rely on a handful of key people including Crean. The biographer Roland Huntford rightly declared that at the worst moments, Crean and Frank Wild – his official deputy – were the only men Shackleton could rely upon.[1] One of the ties that linked Shackleton and Crean was their Irish roots. Shackleton was born in County Kildare and Crean hailed from Kerry, though they came from opposite sides of the social tracks. Shackleton's middle-class roots contrast starkly with those of Crean, who was one of ten children born to a poor Irish farmer during one of Ireland's many famines in the nineteenth century. However, there was a definite bond between the two men, and Frank Worsley, the ship's captain and peerless navigator of the *James Caird*, said that Crean had spent so long with Shackleton that he had become a 'special retainer'. He said Crean and Shackleton often engaged in a 'quaint sort of mimic bickering' which was 'partly chaff and partly a comic revolt against the conditions'. Worsley added: 'As these two watchmates turned in, a kind of rumbling, muttering, growling noise could be heard issuing from the dark & gloomy lair in the bows, sometimes at things in general & sometimes at nothing at all. At times these were so full of quaint conceits and Crean's remarks were so Irish that I ran the risk of explosion by suppressed laughter'.[2] Crean's irrepressible sense of humour and frequent bursts of often tuneless songs provided some important respite for the men as they struggled to stay alive. He was by nature an optimistic man, and many of the officers who commanded Crean recognised the value of raising spirits at moments of great stress, even

Tom Crean's introduction to Polar exploration. The *Discovery* expedition in New Zealand, December 1901 which brought together for the first time some of the famous names of the era. Crean sits in the back row (8th from the left). Also pictured are Ernest Shackleton (front row, 5th left arms folded) and Captain Robert Scott (front, 8th left). Others include Frank Wild (back row 3rd left), William Lashly (back 7th left) and Edgar 'Taff' Evans (back 10th left)

if the critiques of his musical talents were none too flattering. During the open boat *Caird* journey, Shackleton recorded: 'One of the memories that comes to me from those days is of Crean singing at the tiller and nobody ever discovered what song it was. It was devoid of tune and as monotonous as the chanting of a Buddhist monk at his prayers; yet somehow it was cheerful. In moments of inspiration Crean would attempt 'The Wearin' O' the Green'.[3] Worsley was equally bewildered by Crean's musical turns and he had his own memory of the *James Caird* journey, writing: '(Crean) was making noises at the helm that we found by a Sherlock Holmes system of deduction represented The Wearin' O' the Green. Another series of sounds, however, completely baffled us'.[4] Crean was never short of a ready reply, even in the most dire of circumstances. During their first meal on the march across South Georgia, Shackleton joked that Crean had a bigger spoon than his or Worsley's. 'Doesn't

matter, The Skipper (Worsley) has a bigger mouth,' Crean quipped.[5]

Crean was not afraid of responsibility and readily agreed to accept tasks that others found daunting. He was stationed in the *Stancomb-Wills* when the three lifeboats set off for the hazardous trip through the ice to Elephant Island. The *Wills* was the smallest and most vulnerable of the three little vessels and the 'skipper' Hubert Hudson was suffering badly from the ordeal. Crean immediately stepped into the breach, calmly assuming command and steering his colleagues to safety.[6] The *Stancomb-Wills* was frequently threatened by the dangerous waters en route to Elephant Island and the photographer, Frank Hurley recalled: 'It seemed from moment to moment that we should have to...leave her to her fate. Then against the white spume, a dark shape would appear and through the tumult would come faint but cheering, Tom Crean's reassuring hail: 'All well, Sir'.[7] Indeed, it was the *Wills* – with

Shackleton alongside Crean – which made the historic landfall on Elephant Island ahead of the other craft, the *Dudley Docker* and *James Caird*.

Crean's bravery was also evident on Scott's 1910–13 expedition, when he and Apsley Cherry-Garrard and 'Birdie' Bowers were trapped on floating ice and facing certain death by drifting out to sea or being attacked by killer whales. Crean courageously volunteered to go for help, leaping from floe to floe and clambering up the icy shore to summon help for his threatened comrades. There was a carefree, calm assurance about Crean which clearly appealed to Shackleton and other officers who served alongside him during his years in the South. He appeared to have a permanent grin on his face and loved to smoke his pipe. At night on the *James Caird*'s journey to South Georgia, the only visible light was often the red glow from Crean's pipe. An officer from *Discovery* said he was a man with 'a fund of wit and even temper which nothing disturbed'.[8] Tryggve Gran, the young Norwegian who travelled with Scott in 1910–13, remembered the Irishman as a robust, uncompromising character. Gran said he was a man who '...wouldn't have cared if he'd got to the Pole and God Almighty was standing there, or the Devil. He called himself the Wild Man from Borneo and he was'.[9]

Alexander Macklin, a surgeon on *Endurance*, recalled a humorous incident shortly before the expedition left London in the summer of 1914. Queen Alexandra and her entourage came on board to wish the explorers *bon voyage* and Crean was introduced to the glittering array of guests. One of the refined ladies approached Crean and laid a delicate finger on the Irishman's massive chest, asking what the white ribbon on his uniform represented. 'Tom replied: 'That is the Polar Medal.' 'O,' said the lady, 'I thought it was for innocence'. Macklin said it was necessary to be familiar with Tom's 'hard bitten dial' to fully appreciate the irony of the remark.[10] Frank Debenham, a member of Scott's last expedition and founder of the Scott Polar Research Institute in Cambridge, said Crean was in his way a unique person, like a character out of Kipling or Masefield. But there was another side to Tom Crean, which was equally as important to Shackleton. For example, it was Crean who helped keep Shackleton on the straight and narrow during the long frustrating months in South America when they were desperately trying to find a ship to rescue the twenty-two castaways on Elephant Island. It was a highly stressful time and on occasions, Shackleton drowned his sorrows in a bottle, which is hardly surprising. But it was Tom Crean who stood guard over 'The Boss,' protecting him and ensuring that he did not sink too deeply into melancholia. An Englishman in South America at the time witnessed the pair together and wrote that Crean '...seemed to be his bodyguard and would watch over him, even to the extent of warning him not to have a drink'.[12]

Crean remained unendingly cheerful, even after the punishing ordeal of the *Caird* boat journey and crossing of South Georgia to reach the whaling station at Stromness. A photograph of Shackleton, Worsley and Crean taken shortly afterwards shows that Crean is the only man still smiling. He also shared the belief that the three men were supported by a mysterious fourth person in their forced march across South Georgia. Both Shackleton and Worsley wrote afterwards that there was a fourth person in their midst, a story which later inspired the poet T. S. Eliot in writing *The Waste Land*. Worsley said he had a 'strange feeling' about the fourth person and Shackleton confessed that 'Providence guided us'.[13] Tom Crean told Shackleton and Worsley at the time that he also shared the feeling and many years afterwards, he was still maintaining that a guiding hand had assisted the men on their remarkable journey. At home in Ireland, Crean told a friend: 'The Lord brought us home'.[14]

The *Endurance* expedition was the high point of Tom Crean's long and distinguished career in the South, which lasted longer than the careers of almost all other explorers of the age. Only the excellent Frank Wild, who travelled on five expeditions and served on four voyages with Shackleton, spent more of his life in the Antarctic. One telling characteristic was a readiness to volunteer for even the most dangerous of tasks. Indeed, Tom Crean's life as a Polar explorer began voluntarily.

Crean was born in 1877 on a remote hillside farm near the small Irish village of Annascaul on the picturesque Dingle Peninsula, County Kerry. By coincidence, he shared a birthday with another great adventurer of the twentieth century, Sir Edmund Hillary, conqueror of Everest and Antarctic explorer. He was given only a rudimentary education, which provided him with little more than the ability to read and write. At the age of 15 he ran away from home and enlisted in the Royal Navy. For the next eight years, Tom Crean roamed the world in a variety of Queen Victoria's mighty warships. Shortly before Christmas, 1901, his vessel was moored at Lyttelton Harbour, New Zealand, alongside Captain Robert Scott's *Discovery,* which was making last-minute preparations for a two-year expedition to the Antarctic. Then fate stepped in.

The *Endurance* expedition prepares to set sail to the Antarctic, 1914. Crean stands (second left in centre row) with a hand on the rail. Also pictured are Shackleton (centre row, white pullover), Wild (behind) and Worsley (white pullover next to Wild)

One of Scott's sailors attacked a Petty Officer and fled, leaving the expedition a man short. Crean heard about the vacancy and promptly volunteered for a trip into the unknown with Scott. *Discovery* was Crean's Polar apprenticeship and where for the first time he met many of the legendary names of the Heroic Age who were on board the expedition's ship at Lyttelton – Ernest Shackleton, Robert Scott, Frank Wild, Bill Wilson, Edgar Evans and Bill Lashly. Scott also recruited Crean for his next venture on board *Terra Nova*, his tragic last expedition, which set sail in 1910. Crean was a prominent figure in the expedition, man-hauling his sledge to within 150 miles of the South Pole before Scott asked him to turn back. Crean, an emotional man, wept as he said farewell, one of the last men to see Scott and his four companions alive. Months later he was in the party which found Scott's frozen body and he openly wept again.

Crean's perilous 750-mile return to base camp is one of the epic stories of the Heroic Age. The journey, with Lieutenant Evans and Bill Lashly, was a race for life. Their plight worsened when Evans, the sole navigator in the party, developed life-threatening scurvy and had to be carried on the sledge. Evans ordered Crean and Lashly to leave him behind. They refused. Some 35 miles from safety, their strength gave out and Evans was placed in the tent, fully expecting to die. But Crean had other ideas and bravely volunteered to undertake the march single-handed to get help. It was a bold plan since he had no sleeping bag or tent for protection and carried only two sticks of chocolate and three biscuits to eat. Somehow he walked, stumbled and crawled for 18 hours before finally reaching the camp hut. Crean collapsed on the floor of the hut and when revived by a tot of brandy, he promptly volunteered to go back out to rescue his comrades. It was the greatest feat of single-handed bravery from the Heroic Age and Tom Crean was awarded the Albert Medal, the nation's highest recognition for gallantry.

Crean's career exploring the wastes of Antarctica came to an end when the *Endurance* party returned to England in the autumn of 1916. He immediately rejoined the navy and went to war. He finally retired from the navy in 1920 and was soon in demand again when Shackleton was preparing to put together the *Quest* expedition, his own final journey. Shackleton wanted to staff *Quest* with many of his tried and trusted colleagues from *Endurance* and Crean was high on the list. But Tom Crean said no, rejecting his old leader's request with the cheeky remark: 'I have a long haired pal now'.[15] This was a reference to Eileen Herlihy, the woman from his home village whom he had married in 1917. Tom and Eileen had different priorities, largely their three young daughters. In addition, Tom Crean had also gone into business, opening a pub in Annascaul, which he called the South Pole Inn. The pub, which sits alongside a gentle flowing river, still thrives and flourishes to this day; it contains photographs and a cunning trap-door made by a special effects man working on a film nearby, which once opened gives an impression of the noise of a blizzard, to interest the many visitors who drop in for a drink.

Crean was a contented and popular figure in the village. Locals affectionately called him Tom the Pole and Eileen was Nell the Pole. He smoked a pipe all his life, and each day went for a walk with his two dogs, Fido and Toby, who were named after two of the young pups he reared on *Endurance*. One day one of the dogs fell down a cliff and died. Tom Crean, the man who had endured so much in a life of exploration, broke down and cried for the dead animal. His contentment came to an end in the summer of 1938. One day he complained of stomach pains and was rushed to hospital, where appendicitis was diagnosed. But no surgeon was available and Tom Crean was struck down by peritonitis before an operation could be performed. Crean, who had survived a life of unimaginable rigours and danger in his years in the Antarctic, died on July 27, 1938, just a week after his sixty-first birthday. His coffin was carried on the shoulders of his friends and colleagues, and Tom Crean was buried alongside the river which still flows past the South Pole Inn.

Tom Crean never forgot his two famous leaders, Robert Scott and Ernest Shackleton. But he felt differently towards each man. While he was bitterly disappointed at not being selected to go to the South Pole with Scott in 1912, he did not bear a grudge and never criticised the decision. But he undoubtedly felt a closer attachment to Shackleton, perhaps because of their Irish roots. His surviving daughters, Mary and Eileen, say their father respected Scott, but he loved and worshipped Shackleton. Tom Crean made a huge

contribution to Polar exploration yet his accomplishments have been largely overlooked by history. Most people agree that Crean has been not been given the recognition he deserves. However, it is no coincidence that history has been a little unkind to Crean.

The reason is that the well-known figures from the age of Polar exploration – the officers like Scott and Shackleton and the scientists like Wilson – were middle-class characters with the benefit of public school or university education. Ernest Shackleton, who went to Dulwich College in 1887, is a typical example. Writing diaries, letters or even books came easily to these people and as a result they left behind a wealth of written and artistic material for later generations. But Tom Crean did not enjoy the same privilege and his education was very basic. As a result, he left behind very little and only a handful of his letters survive to this day. Tom Crean was a very modest and unassuming man who never courted attention and never gave a single interview to a writer in his life. Contemporaries on his three expeditions all refer to his modesty. Those who knew Tom Crean in later life –

Tom Crean on the day he married Eileen Herily in his home village of Annascaul, Kerry.

including his surviving daughters, Mary and Eileen – all insist that he rarely, if ever, spoke about his exploits in the Antarctic. Those who dropped into the South Pole Inn for a drink and a chat about his adventures were sorely disappointed and invariably left empty-handed.

However, there was also a more unfortunate side to Crean's reluctance to speak about his life. Ireland was in the grip of a bloody civil war when Crean returned home from the Navy in the early 1920s. The battle was between those who supported the partition of Ireland, and the nationalists who remained committed to a united Ireland; Crean was in the middle. Tom Crean's homeland of Kerry had long been a staunch repository of Irish nationalism and despite his fame, Crean found himself in a very difficult position. He was very proud of his Irish roots and spoke the Gaelic language. But he had devoted his life to the British Navy and successive British Polar expeditions, and any association with Britain was, understandably, deeply unpopular in the region. Crean was not an active political figure, but in the circumstances he chose the safest option – he kept his head down and so rarely spoke to anyone about his exploits. Tom Crean, in that sense, was another victim of The Troubles.

Fortunately, we can now speak more freely about the extraordinary and adventurous life of Tom Crean. He was the great unsung hero of Polar exploration and it is time to give him the recognition he fully deserves.

Notes

1   Roland Huntford, *Shackleton*, p. 477.
2   Frank Worsley, *Endurance* diary, Scott Polar Research Institute.
3   Shackleton, *South*, p. 127.
4   Worsley, *Endurance* Diary.
5   Ibid.
6   Michael Smith, *An Unsung Hero: Tom Crean*, Chap. 18.
7   Frank Hurley, *Argonauts of the South*.
8   Albert Armitage, *Two Years in the Antarctic*.
9   Huntford, *Scott and Amundsen*, p. 468.
10   Huntford, *Shackleton*, p. 401.
11   Frank Debenham, 'Tom Crean: An Appreciation', *Polar Record*, 1939.
12   Tom P. Jones, *Patagonian Panorama*, p. 80.
13   Shackleton, *South*, p. 150.
14   Smith, *An Unsung Hero: Tom Crean*, Chap. 22.
15   Recollections of Mary and Eileen Crean O'Brien, quoted in Smith, *Unsung Hero: Tom Crean*, Chap. 26.

Michael Smith is the author of *An Unsung Hero – Tom Crean Antarctic Survivor,* published by The Collins Press, 2000.

Polar veterans. Crean (right) went South three times in 15 years and here poses on board *Endurance* with Alf Cheetham, who sailed on four polar expeditions.

'A Man of Action, and yet a Man of Books':
Shackleton as reader, writer and editor

Jan Piggott
Dulwich College
Curator of *Shackleton: the Antarctic and Endurance*

But the really reckless were fetched
By an older, colder voice, the oceanic whisper:
'I am the solitude that asks and promises nothing;
That is how I shall set you free'.

(W. H. Auden, 'In Praise of Limestone')

Shackleton's four Antarctic expedition ships bear allegorical or emblematic names: *Discovery*; *Nimrod*; *Endurance* and *Quest* (the last name given by his wife, Emily).[1] On the final voyage the brass plaque with Kipling's definition of manhood in the poem 'If', shown in this exhibition, becomes part of the fabric of the actual ship, being actually screwed onto the woodwork under the bridge deck; thus he actually nails, so to speak, his love of literature and its power to teach a code of behaviour to the mast. Sledging pennants attached on bamboo poles to the sledges allude to chivalric codes ('Never the lowered banner, Never the last endeavour' was one of Shackleton's favourite quotations). The headgear of the explorers in the snow, he said, resembled 'an old-time helmet without the visor'.[2] Shackleton in his books recalls even earlier questing motifs or archetypal voyages from mythology deep in Anglo-Saxon consciousness: for example, the *James Caird* and the other two boats moving in such peril between the ice-floes and Elephant Island remind him of 'three Viking ships on the quest of a lost Atlantis'.[3] His sister Alice fancifully associated the root meaning of the place-name Grytviken in South Georgia (where he had once speculated that he might lie in the graveyard with the Norwegian whalers) with her brother Ernest: 'Great Viking'.[4] Shackleton's imagination brought into play a strong sense of allegory and symbolism, and his consciousness (no doubt further educated by his experience as a Mason) naturally engaged with anagogic meanings of experience.

In addressing 'Sir Ernest Shackleton, C.V.O.' in a poem called 'The Knight' John Drinkwater drew on the chivalric code: the explorer is a true knight 'of high descent', a 'soul whipped on by the wander-fire', a quester after 'the shifting golden gleam' who seeks

The call of the secret forces hurled
South of the world, south of the world.

It is no coincidence that Drinkwater uses the Anglo-Saxon compound word 'wander-fire', the verbal device known as a *kenning*; Shackleton's adventures and leadership of his men fit the Anglo-Saxon world of *Beowulf* and 'The Seafarer':

Everything urges the eagerly mooded man to venture on the voyages he
* thinks of,*
The faring over flood, the far bourn.

Shackleton's reading and the connection that he makes between his adventures and literature reveal his inner life. The patterns of what Edwardians liked to call 'the spirit of romance' were laid in his early days – an old tree trunk in the garden at Kilkea House served him as a fantasy ship's cabin; in the Dublin garden behind 35 Marlborough Road he constructed another cabin from a garden frame.[5]

Alice Shackleton wrote to H. R. Mill that as a child her brother was taught to repeat the proverb, 'If at first you don't succeed, try, try again';[6] he habitually used slogans and quotations from his favourite writers, particularly robust lines from Browning expressing a dauntless faith in the essential goodness of things or resilient transformations from negative to positive, from down to up. His two most common quotations from Browning were

There are two points in the adventure of the diver:
One when a beggar he prepares to plunge,
One when a prince he rises with his pearl

from *Paracelsus*, and from 'Prospice'

For sudden the worst turns the best to the brave.

Caspar David Friedrich (1774–1840), *The Wreck of the 'Hope'*, (*Das Eismeer*) 1821. Hamburger Kunsthalle. (Elke Walford, Hamburg)

Under great duress, in real exhaustion and sickness accompanying Scott in the Southern Party towards the Pole on the *Discovery* expedition, one classic expression of determination and endurance in a poem helped him, like a talisman: 'Tennyson's 'Ulysses' keeps running through my head', he wrote in his diary.[7]

Shackleton's own true story moves us likewise today precisely because it corresponds to an archetypal pattern: dispossession of the wooden walls of *Endurance*; the wrecked hopes; the men on the ice-floes, in the three boats and on Elephant Island reduced almost to bare forked animals exposed to the most extreme perils of water, wind, frost and starvation imaginable, but showing superhuman endurance; crossing the uncharted glaciers and mountains of South Georgia and experiencing the sense of super-natural presence. Polar explorers, 'the fellows who go south and north', a character in A. E. W. Mason's novel *The Turnstile* (1912) remarks, 'are the holy men of the

West', who are 'touched by the finger of God'.[8] In an obituary article about Shackleton in 1922 his Belgian brother-in-law, Charles Sarolea, wrote that he was 'the poet and the idealist amongst explorers. He loved exploration for its own sake, because of its romance, because of its moral beauty'. In this respect 'a boy all his life', Shackleton was, he said, 'the representative hero' and 'a patron saint of millions of public school boys'.[9]

Shackleton's famous rallying cry of 'Never the lowered banner, never the last endeavour' is from an unfamiliar source, a chivalric love-poem of two stanzas called 'Cor Cordium' by a Celtic Twilight poet 'Fiona Macleod' (the pseudonym of William Sharp), written between 1900 and 1905, and published in 1907 in *The Hour of Beauty*. Sharp usually wrote poetry that is W. B. Yeats diluted with milk, but one can sense how Shackleton would have been stirred by the poem. He misremembered 'lost endeavour' as 'last endeavour', perhaps as he grew older:

Sweet Heart, true heart, strong heart, star of my life, oh, never
For thee the lowered banner, the lost endeavour!
The weapons are still unforged that thee and me shall dissever,
For I in thy heart have dwelling, and thou hast in mine for ever.

Can a silken cord strangle love, or a steel sword sever?
Or be as a bruisèd reed, the flow'r of joy for ever?
Love is a beautiful dream, a deathless endeavour,
And for thee the lowered banner, O Sweet Heart never!

At Dulwich a school-friend said that that Shackleton 'did very little work, and if there was a scrap he was usually in it';[10] his form positions mostly fell two-thirds of the way down the class. However, there was one apparently capriciously higher form position for Mathematics (ninth out of a class of twenty-two in the Lower Third) and even one freakish second position (out of eighteen) for English History and Literature at Christmas 1889, his last academic year at Dulwich. This indicates a familiar type of pupil, easily bored but with sudden interest and real engagement, the sort of boy whose head is full of more interesting things than those that the teacher has in mind that he should be concentrating on. An incident, one of the few reported from his schooldays, shows the boy dissatisfied with shades of the prison-house and reveals a scientific curiosity that acts as a function of romantic hunger for thoughts that wander through eternity. Harold Begbie in his *Shackleton, a Memory* of 1922 quotes from a statement by Shackleton's form-master for his final year, the Rev. C. E. C. Lefroy, who recalled the year of a transit of Venus:

In the middle of class that morning I noticed that Shackleton had suddenly become invisible when my back had been turned for a moment. Where was he? On the floor, under his desk, observing the transit through a high skylight window. He had calculated that the sun would be in line with him and the skylight window at the right time, so he had brought with him into school a piece of smoked glass for the purpose. This showed an original scientific mind. Not one boy in a thousand would have thought of it.[11]

The only other legend of Shackleton at the College itself – there are several stories of his truancies – is that he climbed over the steep roof of the Great Hall, which was teasingly alluded to in a speech to him at the Alleyn Club Dinner in 5 July 1910: 'I was told about some Antarctic explorer carrying on experiments on the roof of Dulwich College, around the pagoda on the top of the Great Hall. It seems that the explorer mistook that pagoda for the South Pole'.[12]

Both his parents were literary. At meal-times quotation was followed by a demand to identify the source.[13] In an article in *The Captain*, the public school magazine 'for boys and "old boys" ', for April 1910 he reminded his interviewer that he left Dulwich in the Modern Lower Fourth to go to sea, against his father's strong opposition. Though grateful to Dulwich, he said that his first year at sea was his education, and that during that year he learned more of literature than at school: 'I seemed to get at the heart of it then, to see its meaning, to understand its message, and in some degree to catch its spirit'. At Dulwich 'Literature consisted in the dissection, the parsing, the analysing of certain passages from our great poets and prose writers... Teachers should be very careful not to spoil [boys'] taste for poetry for all time by making it a task and an imposition'.[14]

His courtship of Emily Dorman and his marriage obviously took on a poetic pulse from reading, recitation and quotation. The title of his favourite poem, 'Prospice' became a private shibboleth recurring in their letters; even after their deaths the single lapidary optimistic imperative was printed in her funeral Order of Service below her name. It was commonplace in tributes to Shackleton by his contemporaries to record awe at his powers of memory, Orde-Lees, for example, saying that he 'would recite pages and pages of poetry of almost any known poet, many of which he has read through but once or twice'.[15] In his Merchant Navy and White Line days he was notorious for keeping to his cabin and reading.[16]

Expeditions, of course, carried extensive 'Polar Libraries' and, in the ward-room of *Discovery* in the course of a formal debate about the relative merits of Browning and Tennyson, Shackleton as champion of Browning defeated Louis Bernacchi for Tennyson by one vote.[17] Scott, incidentally, took a copy of Browning on his last expedition, and on the polar journey, but according to Apsley Cherry-Garrard, 'I only saw him read it once'.[18]

Hurley noted how after abandoning *Endurance* to the ice, dispossessing his pockets of sovereigns and tossing them into a crack in the ice, Shackleton 'lifted from the dump, that represented the trimmings of civilisation, a pocket volume of Browning', remarking (rather stagily), 'I throw away trash and am rewarded with golden inspirations'.[19] Later the men returned to the ship to secure goods, among them books that included several volumes of *Encyclopædia Britannica*; a small library on the ice was established in Venesta packing cases in the open air-galley behind the cook's windbreak screen.[20]

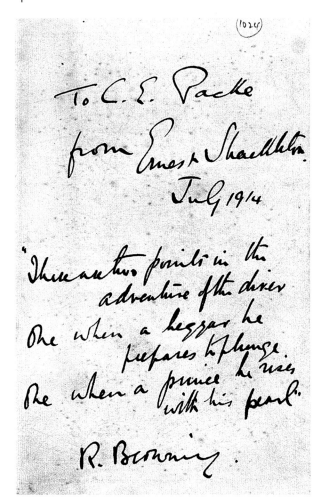

Inscription in a copy of *Shackleton in the Antarctic*, 1911. Dulwich College.

In reading Browning Shackleton responded naturally to his optimism, but also to the ideal in *Paracelsus* of the aspirant who attains wisdom from experience, 'the master-mind, the thinker, the explorer'. Chapter-headings in H. R. Mill's biography of Shackleton (1923) allude to *Paracelsus* in coded form: he transfers the verbs *aspire* and *attain* from Browning's titles to sections of *Paracelsus*, giving the readers of his biography the chapters 'Shackleton aspires' and 'Shackleton attains'. There is a lambent description by Mill of a shipboard conversation with Shackleton about poetry on *Discovery*:

> I always associate Shackleton with the starlight of a summer night in the Bay of Biscay. I had known him for a year before, but it was when he was on watch on the bridge of the *Discovery* from midnight on, as the ship was rolling southward on the first stage of her great voyage, that I discovered his individuality and recognised how he differed in turn of phrase and trend of mind from the other splendid fellows whose names have been made famous by their three years' labours in the Far South. To tell the truth, I was

at first surprised and a little alarmed at the ceaseless flow of quotation from the poets called forth by the summer night, the stars, the phosphorescence of the sea, and the thought of those he left behind him. Nor was it altogether pleasing to find that this young sailor was already familiar with every reference which rose to my mind from books I had read years before his thoughts had turned that way, and with many which I had never seen; one exception only do I remember, which he seized upon with an amusing avidity. I feared that he was something of a dreamer, for such absorbing literary instincts savoured of the unpractical; but this fear was a liar, as I soon discovered.[21]

In 1909 when Shackleton visited the Browning Settlement in Camberwell, a philanthropic institute in a deprived area called after Robert Browning, he claimed kinship with workers, 'ever since he shovelled coal at Iquique', and claimed that here he found himself 'in touch both with reality and poetry as he never was at the grand Society functions'.[22] Elected President of the Settlement in 1914 when bound for the South, he promised to name a mountain after the poet 'if he should discover new peaks'.[23] Addressing the Poetry Society at the Hotel Cecil in October 1911 on 'Poetry and Active Life' Shackleton said that sailors have wider horizons, and their experience of nature face to face therefore trains them 'to feel what only poets can say'. He told his audience that real help was given to his men by studying great poetry, and remarked how 'those who were least educated' often expressed the truest thoughts' in their own poems.[24] The *Daily Chronicle* on August 4th, 1916 in an article, 'Full Story of Small Boats' Terrible Voyage; Three Members of the Crew back in London', reported that after the loss of the well-equipped library of *Endurance* 'only a few personal pocket volumes survived. Among them were two 'Brownings', Sir Ernest carried one... Mr. McNish, the carpenter, had the other, and he is a Scotsman'. Scientific pages from the *Encyclopædia Britannica*, on the other hand, were useful for cigarette papers.

During the *Nimrod* expedition on the Southern Journey in appalling conditions, Shackleton was carrying Shakespeare's comedies, and his diary records that he was reading *Much Ado about Nothing* and *The Taming of the Shrew* in his tent, and just before turning back he was reading aloud *The Merchant of Venice*.[25] During 'the stress and strain' of a furious gale 'Browning's verse was often the subject of conversation'.[26] On the ice during the *Endurance* expedition he read Kinglake's *Eothen*.[27]

Shackleton's range of reference includes Byron, Shelley, the Book of Job, obviously 'The Ancient Mariner' (a copy of which was taken with them on the ice-floe after *Endurance* sank), Kipling and the Canadian Robert Service, the poet of the Lone Trail, who wrote of 'the brotherhood of men who know the South' and 'the stark and sullen solitudes that sentinel the Pole'. In newspaper interviews Shackleton quotes Keats.[28] Shackleton also responded deeply to the popular literature of pilgrim souls: his favourite hymn was 'Lead, kindly Light', according to the printed *Order of Service* for his Memorial at Eastbourne. He also particularly liked a school song from Victoria College, Wellington, New Zealand, that celebrated 'the long white road' and the heart 'that never swerves'. A piece of paper with this quotation on it (by a slight irony, written out by Emily) is shown in the current exhibition. Shackleton carried printed copies of Kipling's 'If' (one of them is also shown) to give to likely souls. Conrad was a favourite novelist (*Typhoon* comes to mind).

Shackleton is heir to early nineteenth-century romantic attitudes, particularly in his sympathy with the cult of the restless fugitive from urban civilisation, and the figure of the explorer as a sage. We know that a favourite book of his childhood was Jules Verne's *Twenty Thousand Leagues under the Sea*, and he took as his pseudonym the name of the hero Nemo in his courtship of Emily;[29] also as 'Nemo' he signed his writings in the *South Polar Times* and the *Aurora Australis*.

Shackleton's Prose

The world now seems to apprehend the *Endurance* expedition through Hurley's genius by his photographs and the film *South*. Shackleton's own writings, however, are not only stirring both in epic narrative and in images, but use a truly poetic style that avoids cosmetic flourish. Orde-Lees wrote in his *Endurance* diary that '*The Heart of the Antarctic* is the only book in use throughout Holland officially as an English reader in all the schools, it having been chosen at once for literary style and descriptive writing'.[30] Shackleton certainly profited from his association with the ghost-writer Edward Saunders, whom he met in New Zealand. In the Preface to *The Heart of the Antarctic* Shackleton calls him his 'secretary' who 'advised him on literary points'.[31] *South* is evidently more of Shackleton's own work than sceptics would like to believe, though Saunders had a fairly large part in it, and Leonard Hussey was the final editor.[32] In Saunders' letter to Leonard Tripp of 10 August 1922, in which he begs him not to let the public know how much Shackleton's style owed to him, Saunders reveals real awe for Shackleton's powers of description in dictating to him his recollections

of extreme dangers.[33] Some extraordinarily lyrical passages are found in the diaries, unembellished by Saunders. A supreme example is this extract from *The Heart of the Antarctic*, which after quoting 'The Ancient Mariner' and describing erratic puffs of wind, reads

> It is as though we were at the world's end, and were bursting in on the birthplace of the clouds and the resting home of the four winds, and one has a feeling that we mortals are being watched with a jealous eye by the forces of nature.[34]

Certainly there was a tradition of graphic description of sublime and beautiful polar landscapes before Coleridge's 'Ancient Mariner', in the source books of polar journeys which we know (from John Livingston Lowes's *The Road to Xanadu*) that Coleridge studied for the details of the poem. The genre had become fairly sophisticated by the time of James Fennimore Cooper's *The Sea Lions* of 1849, as in this description of the effect of sunshine on icebergs:

> that which had so lately been black and frowning was, as by the touch of magic, suddenly illuminated and became bright and gorgeous, throwing out its emerald hues, or perhaps a virgin white, that filled the beholder with delight, even amid the terrors and dangers by which, in very truth, he was surrounded.[35]

Shackleton described the icescapes of the Barrier and the Weddell Sea with the bergs and floes in terms of fantastic architecture: 'a deserted town, built of the purest alabaster, with its edifices crumbling under the seasons, and its countless unpeopled streets, avenues and alleys'.[36] To Hurley they seemed a surreal phantasmagoric Venice with gondolas of ice.[37] Here is a bravura chromatic passage from *The Heart of the Antarctic*:

> The sunsets at the beginning of April were wonderful; arches of prismatic colours, crimson and golden-tinged clouds, hung in the heavens nearly all day, for time was going on and soon the sun would have deserted us. The days grew shorter and shorter, and the twilight longer. During these sunsets the western mountains stood out gloriously and the summit of Erebus was wrapped in crimson when the lower slopes had faded into grey. To Erebus and the western mountains our eyes turned when the end of the long night grew near in the month of August, for the mighty peaks are the first to catch up and tell the tale of the coming glory and the last to drop the crimson mantle from their high shoulders as night draws on. Tongue and pencil would sadly fail in attempting to describe the magic of the colouring in the days when the sun was leaving us. The very clouds at this time were iridescent with rainbow hues. The sunsets were poems. The change from twilight into night, sometimes lit by a crescent moon, was extraordinarily

beautiful, for the white cliffs gave no part of their colour away, and the rocks beside them did not part with their blackness, so the effect of deepening night over these contrasts was singularly weird. In my diary I noted that throughout April hardly a day passed without an auroral display. On more than one occasion the auroral showed distinct lines of colour, merging from a deep red at the base of the line of light into a greenish hue on top. About the beginning of April the temperature began to drop considerably, and for some days in calm, still weather the thermometer often registered 40° below.[38]

If one was compiling an anthology of Antarctic writing one would include, for comparison with Shackleton, a passage from Apsley Cherry-Garrard's *The Worst*

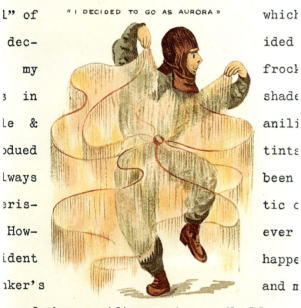

'I decided to go as Aurora', vignette by Edward Wilson from the *South Polar Times*, Vol III, p. 119.

The Aurora Australis was described by Thomas Orde-Lees in his *Endurance* diary as 'a wide band across the sky' with 'second and third bands concentric to the first'. 'All the while the glow is a greenish white similar to the flurescence [sic] in an x-ray tube. Later the arcs begin to form what look like hanging curtains of glowing light and then change their shape, at times so rapidly, that it gives the appearance of waving curtains' (19 April 1915, p. 109, Dartmouth College Library).

Journey in the World: here he is describing the glaciers on the southern slopes of Erebus:

> Visualize a torrent ten miles long and twenty miles broad; imagine it falling over mountainous rocks and tumbling over itself in giant waves; imagine it arrested in the twinkling of an eye, frozen and white. Countless blizzards have swept their drifts over it, but have failed to hide it. And it continues to move. As you stand in the still cold air you may sometimes hear the silence broken by the sharp reports as the cold contracts or its own weight splits it. Nature is tearing up that ice as human beings tear paper.[39]

At a climax of tense heroic duress Shackleton's style tends to become sharp and sinewy, and mimetic of physical movement and strain:

> Three bergs were in sight, and we pulled towards them, hoping that a trail of brash would be floating on the sea to leeward; but they were hard and blue, devoid of any sign of cleavage, and the swell that surged around them as they rose and fell made it impossible to approach closely. The wind was gradually hauling ahead, and as the day wore on the rays of the sun beat fiercely down from a cloudless sky on pain-racked men. Progress was slow, but gradually Elephant Island came near.[40]

This physicality in the style is shown again in describing dire peril on the *James Caird*: 'Deep seemed the valleys where we lay between the reeling seas. High were the hills when we perched momentarily on the tops of giant combers'.[41] Shackleton is seldom aphoristic, but when he is, echoes of Browning, or in this case, *King Lear* often appear in his prose:

> Man can sustain life with very scanty means. The trappings of civilization are soon cast aside in the face of stern realities, and given the barest opportunity of winning food and shelter, man can live and even find his laughter ring true.[42]

At high points the writing is sublime:

> The temperature was down to 4° below zero, and a film of ice formed on the surface of the sea. When we were not on watch we lay in each other's arms for warmth. Our frozen suits thawed where our bodies met, and as the slightest movement exposed these comparatively warm spots to the biting air, we clung motionless, whispering each to his companion our hopes and thoughts. Occasionally from an almost clear sky came snow-showers, falling silently on the sea and laying a thin shroud of ice over our bodies and our boats.[43]

The equivalent description of an epiphany in *South* to match the passage quoted above from *The Heart of the Antarctic* about 'the birthplace of the clouds' is a meditation on the exhausted arrival of the three at

Stromness after the trek across South Georgia, carrying only the adze, the cooker shown in this exhibition and the log-book:

> That was all, except our wet clothes, that we brought out of Antarctica, which we had entered a year and a half before with a well-found ship, full equipment, and high hopes. That was all of tangible things; but in memories we were rich. We had 'suffered, starved, and triumphed, grovelled down yet grasped at glory, grown bigger in the bigness of the whole.' We had seen God in his splendours, heard the text that Nature renders. We had reached the naked soul of man.[44]

Shackleton was said to be an exceptional orator; one can understand the famous effect on his audiences from the patriotic rhetoric of the pamphlet 'Sir Ernest Shackleton's stirring Appeal', a speech given in Sydney on 20 March 1917, after the *Endurance* expedition, encouraging men to join up with the Australian Imperial Force. In the course of the speech as visual recruiting rhetoric he waved the Union Flag given by the king to the expedition which 'had flown over many a barren ice field and upon Elephant Island'. He shared with his audience memories of 'the quiet hours of the night, when you think over the little snakes of doubt twisting in your heart. I have known them'; he surely stirred a response in the audience to his appeal to the qualities of endurance needed by all recruits:

> We lived long days in the South. The danger of the moment is a thing easy to meet, and the courage of the moment is in every man at some time. But I want to say that we lived through slow dead days of toil, of struggle, dark striving and anxiety; days that called not for heroism in the bright light of day, but simply for dogged persistent endeavour to do what the soul said was right. It is in that same spirit that we of the British race have to face this war.

Shackleton's Poetry

Taken as a body, Shackleton's poems, which after his death were once or twice proposed to be published, are not quite so impressive, and they seem more derivative than his prose. They reveal his temperament clearly, however, and rise to real power. In his late teens he was writing quest poems, and at the age of twenty-one he wrote a visionary poem, 'A Tale of the Sea,' about gales and cursing sailors and the heroes of the White Ensign:

> *Oh! the deepest blue of the sky:*
> *Oh! the greenest sward of the lea:*
> *To me seem dull and paltry,*
> *Since I dreamed of that tossing sea,*
> *For now I know it is peopled*

> *With wandering souls of the past:*
> *Blown to & fro on its surface*
> *At the mercy of every blast.*[45]

'L'Envoi' from the *South Polar Times* for 1903 celebrates companionship, and records telling sensory detail of sledging:

> *The chafe of the strap on the shoulder; the whine of the dogs as they go...*
> *The wind-blown furrows and snow drifts; the crystal's play in the light.*[46]

'Erebus', printed in *Aurora Australis* (pseudonymously signed 'Nemo') pictures 'weird gloom' and polarises the volcano against the cold – fire and smoke opposed to ice and snow:

> *At your head the swinging smoke-cloud; at your feet the grinding floes;*
> *Racked and seared by the inner fires, gripped close by the outer snows.*[47]

Shackleton as Editor

At the age of twenty-six as Third Officer on a Boer War troopship, in conjunction with the Surgeon, Shackleton wrote and published '*O. H. M. S.*,' *an Illustrated Record of*

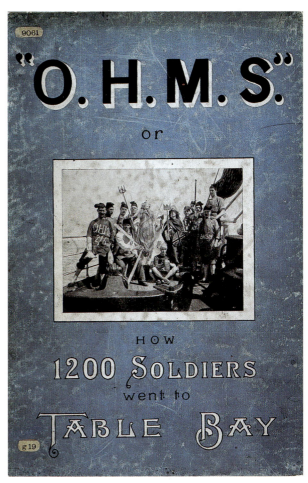

'*O. H. M. S.*', 1900 (**No. 16**)
(By permission of the British Library. 9061 g.19 W).

the Voyage of S. S. 'Tintagel Castle', carrying twelve hundred soldiers from Southampton to Cape Town, March 1900. The book carried an epigraph from Kipling, 'Troopin', Troopin', Troopin', to the Sea'; it aimed to show faithfully the life of a soldier on a Boer War troopship. The book is interesting for its resonant imperial sentences: 'When the kits are unbuckled and the rifles laid by, when we can look again on the whitening fields of corn, and around our hearths we hear the music of well-loved voices, then we will have done our work as men, and made for our Queen another Wef to add to her great Empire'.[48] It also reveals what Shackleton learned about not lowering the banner, about keeping up the morale of men very likely doomed: he organised semaphoring classes and stage-managed entertainments such as the Father Neptune ceremony on crossing the line, shown on the cover. He seems fascinated by statistical lists – the passengers included 99 game-keepers and 17 'gentlemen' – and by the inventory of stores – 2,800 lbs. of Golden Syrup and 25,000 cigarettes.

Shackleton must have been in the eyes of the men on the *Discovery* expedition the ideal editor of the *South Polar Times*, as he was elected sole editor. The atmos-

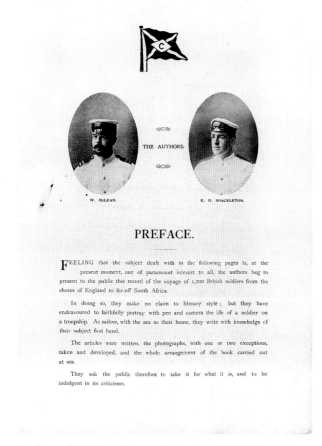

PREFACE.

Preface to *O. H. M. S.* (By permission of the British Library.)

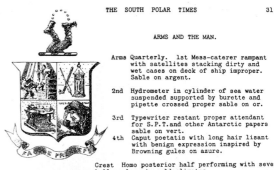

'Arms and the Man', *The South Polar Times,* Vol. I, iii, June 1902, p. 31.

phere of the editorial office sounds like a study in a boys' public school.[49] The satirical version of Shackleton's coat of arms that appeared in Vol. I of the *South Polar Times* teased him affectionately for his literary interests, caricaturing him as a poet in the style of Gilbert and Sullivan's Bunthorne, the absurd Wildean figure in *Patience*. For this periodical he wrote rather stilted, forced and self-conscious editorials typical of an Edwardian schoolboy, and some poems. When he came to edit *Aurora Australis* eight years later on the *Nimrod* expedition, and wrote a preface recalling his work on the *South Polar Times* he must also have recalled his youthful work on 'O. H. M. S.' In planning the *Aurora* he perhaps realised how for a midwinter publication he could outdo the Scott expedition with its typewritten magazine by bringing the first printing press to Antarctica. In the case of *Aurora Australis* the contents of the magazine are not so admirable as the vehicle, with the exception of Shackleton's own poem 'Erebus', and Marston's etchings and lithographs.

It was a bold gesture to bring an Albion Press into the hut at Cape Royds; to trust in a three weeks' apprenticeship for Joyce and Wild at Sir Joseph Causton and Sons Ltd., and to print ('At the Sign of the Penguins') in cramped and crowded conditions in which the blizzard raged outside, the floor was filthy, the ink froze and smuts from the blubber and coal stove settled on the paper. George Marston used to have to print the lithographs in the early hours of the morning while the others slept. Polar ennui was defeated, and a fine work of printing was achieved in distinguished Caslon Old Face type. The book had an inventive and witty binding (which incorporated for the inside back board of the book an original side of the Venesta storage cases stencilled with the name of the food it contained, so that

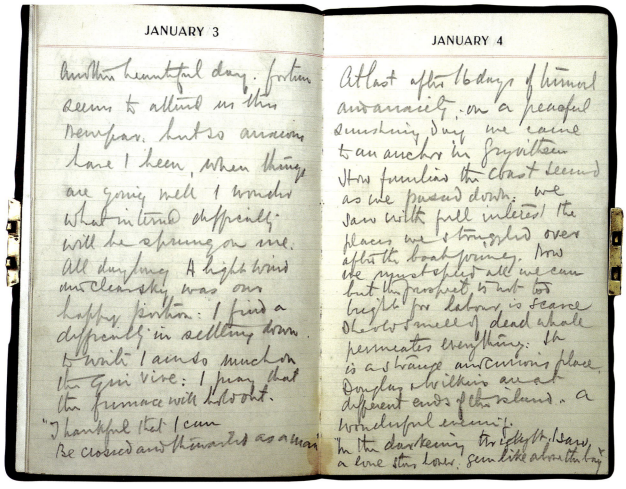

JANUARY 3

JANUARY 4

Shackleton's Diary on the *Quest* expedition, written the night that he died. (**No. 72**)

you have the 'petit pois' copy, for example). Thus Shackleton created a bibliophile's rarity and a supply of mementos for his rich and famous associates.

In Shackleton's questing, enduring idealist mentality, that sought among the void spaces 'some of the scenery and the sight of the great mountains whose stern peaks dare the stars, which have never been seen by eye of mortal man before',[50] his profound love of books and the word seems involved at a very deep level with his actions. In a magazine article of 1920 Gerald Cumberland wrote of Shackleton that he was 'a man of action and yet a man of books'. He used an arresting metaphor in describing the man: he had 'the sea's restless energy, its buoyancy, its salt healthiness, and something of its mystery'.[51] Testing the salinity of water on *Discovery* for Shackleton was a chore, but whispering lines of Browning to his tent-companions with a blizzard outside engaged his soul. Who that knows the story of Shackleton can read the last two pages of his diary, written alone in his cabin on the *Quest* at

Grytviken, about the 'lone star hovering Gem-like above the bay'[52] without being deeply stirred?

Notes

1   Frank Wild, *Shackleton's Last Voyage*, 1923, p. 8.
2   E. H. Shackleton, *The Heart of the Antarctic*, 1909, II, p. 158.
3   Ernest Shackleton, *South*, 1919, p. 135.
4   Alice Shackleton to H. R. Mill, 8 July 1922. Scott Polar Research Institute, MS 100/113/2; D. The Norwegian roots of *Grytviken* mean a prosaic 'stewpan bay'.
5   Kilkea: see n. 4; Dublin: H. R. Mill, *The Life of Sir Ernest Shackleton*, 1923, p. 20.
6   See n. 3 above.
7   11 January 1903. Quoted in M. & J. Fisher, *Shackleton*, 1957, p.66.
8   Op. cit., p. 252.
9   'Sir Ernest Shackleton: a Study in Personality', *The Contemporary Review*, CXXI, Jan.-June, 1922, p. 325.
10 O. T. Burne to H. R. Mill, May 10, 1922. Scott Polar Research Institute, MS 100/17; D.
11 Op. cit., p. 15.
12 'Alleyn Club', Speech by H. J. Powell, *The Alleynian*, XXXVIII, July 1910, p. 327.
13 Mill, 1923, p. 21.

14 ('How I began. Sir Ernest Shackleton') XXIII, April 1910, pp. 42–43.

15 Op. cit., July 28, 1915, p. 209. Special Collections Library, Dartmouth College, Hanover, New Hampshire, Stef. MSS/185.

16 Fisher, p. 10.

17 Mill, p. 70.

18 *The Worst Journey in the World*, (1922), 1937 ed., p. 199.

19 Frank Hurley, *Argonauts of the South*, p. 192.

20 Alfred Lansing, *Endurance*, (1959), 1999, p. 80.

21 'Ernest Henry Shackleton, M.V.O.', *Travel and Exploration*, II, 7, July 1909, p. 2.

22 Mill, p. 163.

23 Ibid., p. 199.

24 *The Times*, 28 Oct. 1911, p. 11.

25 E. H. Shackleton, *The Heart of the Antarctic*, I, p. 270. Cf. Frank Wild's diary for 7 January, 1909, quoted in Leif Mills, *Frank Wild*, Whitby, 1999, p. 98.

26 Ibid., p. 49.

27 Huntford, p. 464.

28 *Daily Mail*, 31 December 1913; *Answers*, 10 January, 1914.

29 Fisher, p. 5.

30 Op. cit., 28 July 1915. See n. 15.

31 Op. cit., I, p. x.

32 Huntford, p. 673.

33 Scott Polar Research Institute, MS 367/19; D.

34 Op. cit., I, p. 289.

35 Op. cit., II, p. 107.

36 *The Heart of the Antarctic*, II, p. 253. Frank Worsley, *Endurance*, 1931, pp. 8–9, also speaks of the ice-floes as a 'marvellous city of ice', and says that 'many of us would not have been surprised had we been hailed by voices'. Later this is extended to 'a dazzling city of cathedral spires, domes, minarets'. p. 43.

37 Frank Hurley, *Argonauts of the South*, 1925, p. 42: 'crystal gondolas drifted on blue canals through the ruins of marble cities'.

38 Op. cit., I, p. 222.

39 Op. cit., (1922), 1937 ed., p. 185.

40 *South*, p. 138.

41 Ibid., p. 166.

42 Ibid., p. 123.

43 Ibid., pp.133–4.

44 V. C. ibid., p. 36.

45 Fisher, pp. 497–8.

46 Ibid., p. 501.

47 Ibid., p. 502.

48 Op. cit., p. 47.

49 Fisher, p. 42.

50 E. H. Shackleton, *Adventure*, 1928, p. 20.

51 'The World Celebrity of the Week. No. 59. Sir Ernest Shackleton'. Press cutting from unidentified journal, April 3, 1920.

52 January 4, 1922. Frank Wild, *Shackleton's Last Voyage*, p. 59.

Gustave Doré, illustration for *The Ancient Mariner* (detail).

Norman Wilkinson

CATALOGUE by Jan Piggott

The *James Caird*

NOTE: measurements are given in centimetres, height before width

1 THE 'JAMES CAIRD'
Dulwich College

The *James Caird*, a whale-boat or 'whaler', was much the most seaworthy of the three lifeboats salvaged from the crushed *Endurance*. A life-boat is to be seen in the photograph in the exhibition of the *Polaris* newly arrived from Sandefjord at the South West India Docks in London in July 1914. Two life-boats were part of the original Norwegian equipment of the ship, but the

James Caird was specially commissioned in London. The three boats were, of course, with the men for the five and a half months on the ice between the destruction of the *Endurance* and the landing on Elephant Island. The ship also carried a fourth boat, a motor-boat, whose screw and exhaust-pipe are visible in some photographs and in Frank Hurley's film *South*, but there are few references to it; from the film, where it is to be seen at a very late stage in the crushing of *Endurance,* it seems likely that this boat was abandoned on the wreck.

The *James Caird* weighed over a ton, and was hauled by the men over the ice on sledges in relays for about 60 yards at a time, with the utmost difficulty and misery.[1] The photograph of the boat displayed in Selfridges roof garden in 1920 shows a sign attached to the stem saying that the holes in it were 'for straps to give purchase when hauling boat over ice blocks'. At first the ordinary sledges were used, but then Shackleton had Henry McNeish the expedition carpenter make stronger ones.

Harry McNeish was the son of a bootmaker from Port Glasgow, although the literature says that he came from Dundee. McNeish signed his name Harry Macnish, though members of his family today say it is spelled McNish; again, the standard spelling in Antarctic literature is McNeish. He had worked for twenty-three years as a carpenter in the Royal Navy before

The *James Caird* in the North Cloister at Dulwich College.

Preceding pages: **3** Details from Norman Wilkinson, *An Epic of the Sea*.

After the Endurance was crushed, the men tried in vain to drag their lifeboats over the ice to open water (**155 r**).

The reproduction *James Caird*, built for the IMAX film *Shackleton's Antarctic Adventure* by Bob Wallace (who plays Shackleton) and by Andy Fletcher, photographed by Andy Fletcher off South Georgia.

working on the construction of *Discovery*. He immediately afterwards joined the expedition as a carpenter, and spent much of the expedition on the ship at Hut Point.

The sledge-runners kept freezing into the ice while the men hauled the other boats in turn. Under Frank Wild's supervision they pulled for four days, and then for seven days.[2] It was such heavy going, encountering pressure ridges as much as two stories high, that they slept by day and travelled by night when the snow was hardest.[3] She was eventually launched on 9 April 1916 and perilously navigated – though there was laughter and singing at times – through leads among the pack-ice in the Weddell Sea, and then in the open sea for the landing at Elephant Island.

The boat had no name until all three boats were named in a ceremony on the ice on 26 November 1915. George Marston painted the name on her.[4] The boat has since been repainted and given a commonplace sign-writer's lettering. In photographs of the boat in her early years after her return to England she appears,

more romantically, bleached like a bone on the beach. The three boats were all originally painted white, as was conventional for a lifeboat and as of course they are shown in Hurley's photographs. George Marston's paintings featuring the *Caird* show her with a brown upper strake. The men were fearful when traversing the leads between the ice-floes that killer whales would mistake the white bottom of the boat with the men on it for ice and seals, and topple them over.[5]

The advantages of whalers in the Antarctic had been recognised for a long time, as is shown by this passage published in 1849 in James Fennimore Cooper's *The Sea Lions, or the Lost Sealers*:

> A whale-boat differs from the ordinary jolly-boat, launch, or yawl – gigs, barges, dinguis, &c., &c., being exclusively for the service of vessels of war – in the following particulars, viz. :- It is sharp at both ends, in order that it may 'back off,' as well as 'pull on'; it steers with an oar, instead of a rudder, in order that the bows may be thrown round to avoid danger when not in motion; it is buoyant, and made to withstand the shock of waves at both ends; and it is light and shallow, though strong, that it may be pulled with

facility. When it is remembered that one of these little egg-shells – little as vessels, though of good size as boats – is often dragged through troubled waters at the rate of ten or twelve knots, and frequently at even a swifter movement, one can easily understand how much depends on its form, buoyancy, and strength. Among seamen, it is commonly thought that a whale-boat is the safest craft of the sort in which men can trust themselves in rough water.[6]

The *James Caird* was built in the yard of Messrs. W. and J. Leslie on the Isle of Dogs to the east of the West India Docks. The best description of her is by Frank Worsley, who commissioned and designed her:

> Her length was 22 feet 6 inches, beam 6 feet, depth 3 feet 6 inches. She was double-ended and clinker-built to my orders in July, 1914, by Messrs. W. J. Leslie of Coldharbour, Poplar. Her planking was Baltic pine, keel and timbers American elm, stem and sternpost English oak. She was more lightly built than is required by the Board of Trade. This made her springy and buoyant. To make room for men and stores we removed the Muntz metal tanks fitted in her as a lifeboat.
>
> While drifting on the pack-ice, after the loss of the *Endurance*, the carpenter had built her 15 inches higher, constructed a whale-back at each end and fitted a pump made from the Flinders bar casing of the ship's compass. We launched the boat into a pool and loaded her with two and a third tons' weight – about the same as on the great journey, which left her with 2 feet 2 inches freeboard, *i.e.*, height above water.[7]

Worsley makes an odd mistake, describing her as 'clinker-built' (where the strakes overlap), as she is certainly 'carvel-built' (flush and smooth). Unlike the whaler described by Fennimore Cooper, the *James Caird* of course had a rudder, which was dislodged by the rocks at the end of the Boat Journey, and which by a curious trick of providence was returned after six days by the sea at their feet in the cove. The other two boats were cutters, which have a normal stem and transom-stern. In the same ceremony all three boats were named after sponsors of the expedition: one of the cutters became the *Dudley Docker* (of the Birmingham firm British Small Arms, who paid for the *Endurance*), and the other the *Stancomb-Wills* after Dame Janet Stancomb-Wills of Margate (an adopted member of the Wills tobacco family, who was a philanthropic admirer of Shackleton). 'What names!', Hurley wrote in his diary.[8]

The *James Caird* herself was named after the most generous backer of the expedition, Sir James Caird of Dundee, a widower who had lost his only child. He had an immense fortune through the jute trade, employing 300 people in his works. To Dundee he gave hospitals and a sanatorium, and had recently given a Town Hall costing £100,000, for which George V laid the foundation stone. He also endowed the Caird Insect House at the London Zoo. To Shackleton Caird gave £24,000 absolutely without conditions; other backers had insisted on pledges and loans. According to H. R. Mill, Caird said, 'Do you think, Sir Ernest, that those gentlemen would release you from that obligation if you were to tell them that there was a man in Scotland who would find the remaining twenty-four thousand pounds on that condition?'.[9] One of Shackleton's first acts on the *Endurance* expedition, on 16 January 1915, was to name newly discovered land sighted from the ship the Caird Coast.

Before they took to the boats McNeish raised the gunwale ten inches by adding chafing battens from wood salvaged from *Endurance* to her bow, 'to keep the young ice from cutting through as she is built of white pine which won't last long in ice'.[10] The caulking was done with cotton lamp-wick and with oil paints sacrificed by Marston, finished off with seal's blood.[11]

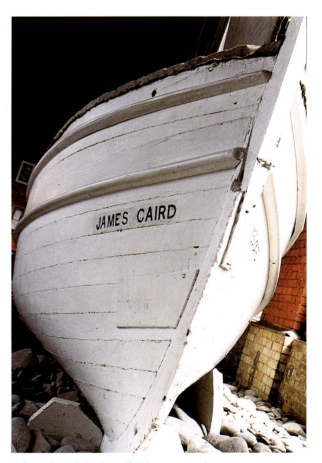

A bow view of the *James Caird*.

Arrived on Elephant Island, Macklin wrote in his diary, they 'began to cut Caird down, she being so heavy we could not handle her or haul her clear of surf. Noon, hauled boat well clear of surf. Cooked old albatross: very good but a little tough'.[12] McNeish mended a hole made by a sharp spur of ice in the passage through the ice-floes[13] on the starboard bow above the waterline 'with a small patch of metal',[14] and strengthened her for the Boat Journey by bolting the mast of the *Stancomb-Wills* inside the *Caird* along the keel. McNeish, who at forty-eight, was the eldest member of the crew, was a brilliant craftsman: he had such a good eye he was said seldom to measure a piece of wood.[15] He wrote in his diary, 'I have only a saw, hammer & chisel & adze but we are managing all right'.[16] Notwithstanding his endearing qualities he was disliked by Thomas Orde-Lees, who referred in his dairy to 'the objectionable cantankerous carpenter, who was so grossly insubordinate to Capt. Worsley when hauling the boats that Sir Ernest found it expedient to call a muster & read over the ship's articles'.[17]

Since there was not enough wood to make a deck, McNeish added a canvas top to the boat to limit the amount of baling the men would have to do, supported by sledge-runners and pieces of Venesta board (three-ply wood made with waterproof glue) from the food cases.[18] In his diary he wrote, 'Cheetham and McCarthy have been busy trying to stretch the canvas for the deck. They had rather a job as it was frozen stiff'. The frozen bolt of canvas, McNeish said, was thawed, foot by foot, over the blubber stove, allowing the brittle needles to be pushed and pulled through the heavy fabric with a pair of pincers.[19] Worsley said that Greenstreet was actually the best at this work, accompanying it with his 'cheerful profanity'.[20] 'Heavy, wet snow fell throughout the day as they worked, and Wild, of all people, was heard to say that if the weather continued much longer "some of the party will undoubtedly go under" '.[21] This became the slippery canvas top, referred to as 'flimsy' by Worsley,[22] and as 'more like stage-scenery' by Orde-Lees[23] over which amid the appalling waters on the Boat Journey they crawled and hung to the mast, the waves sweeping over them, in order to chip off the ice.[24] Worsley said that 'we all agreed it was the worst job we had ever taken on in our lives'.[25] For the rigging the lug-sail from the *Stancomb-Wills* had already been cut down at Ocean Camp to make a mizzen sail for the *Caird*; the small mizzen mast of the *Stancomb-Wills* had been cut down at the same time to be put on the *Caird*. The *Caird* already had a

mainsail and a jib. In Harding Dunnett's words, 'she was rigged as a ketch, with a jib, a standing lug-sail with a loose foot (i.e. no boom) on the mainmast and a standing lugsail, but with a boom, on the mizzen mast'.[26] Ballast of boulders, shingle and sand was put in canvas bags or blankets. Shackleton and Worsley did not agree about the amount of ballast or the rigging, but Shackleton took the responsibility for the decisions. Worsley, indeed, thought that Shackleton had put twice as much ballast as was necessary in the *Caird*, and that this made the boat too stiff and jumpy; Shackleton later admitted this to him and apologised: 'Not every leader, after he had brought his men safely through, would have conceded that he had made even a small mistake'.[27] Worsley said of the evening before they left that

> they tell me that I seemed cheery enough that night, and I am glad that I appeared so, for I certainly did not feel it. I was haunted by a series of pictures which flashed across my mind, pictures of what would become of these men should our attempt fail. I looked on their faces, and although to other eyes, I daresay, those faces, grimy and bearded, would not have seemed handsome or lovable, I felt as though I could not get my fill of gazing at them.[28]

Each Saturday the marooned men on Elephant Island were to toast 'the Boss and crew of the *James Caird*' in melted ice, methylated spirit and ginger from the medical chest.[29]

The story of the Boat Journey is now too well known to rehearse here, but it is worth recalling that Shackleton's biographer Roland Huntford noted how 'at the misty centre of Shackleton's dream lay an epic voyage in an open boat'.[30] During the *Nimrod* expedition Shackleton had a light portable boat, the *Raymond*, named after his eldest son, which he thought of dragging across the entire continent to cross the Weddell Sea to rejoin *Nimrod*. In this boat Wild and Marston later went on a jaunt up the west coast of Scotland. Shackleton on the same expedition also thought of sailing to New Zealand in the *Raymond* in case no boat returned the following year.[31] The appalling discomfort of the journey has perhaps not been emphasised enough: into the sleeping place in the bows, seven feet by five, they painfully burrowed in the dark, lying on top of cases of food, the boulders and the bags of shingle. Shackleton himself had to direct the operation of getting in and out of their sleeping-bags. 'Within the bowels of the boat our unfortunate bodies were swung up and banged down on mountainous seas as we rushed up hills and plunged down valleys, shivering as we were slung from side to side of the boat'.³² They woke up half-smothered in their bags, and Worsley recalls sensations of being buried alive on waking. For cooking they put their backs against the sides of the boat opposite to each other and held the Primus between their feet, supporting the 'cooker', the hoosh pot, above the Primus.³³ Worsley said that the worst feature was the moulting reindeer hairs from their sleeping-bags which got into their eyes, noses and mouths and into the hoosh.³⁴

There is a telling detail in Worsley's account of their days camped at King Haakon Bay: after describing the miraculous drinking on their knees from the fresh water of the stream, Worsley says that he and Shackleton explored the grim lonely beach of King Haakon Sound, and Shackleton picked up a child's toy boat, 'some child's lost treasure', among wreckage. Both this detail and the image of a graveyard of wreckage from ships that they found closer to the *Caird* – teak and brass, masts, figureheads, binnacles, broken oars – seem as a parallel and in the context of the Boat Journey to take on an ironic symbolic meaning.³⁵

After the Boat Journey the *Caird* was towed off by the Norwegian whalers and hoisted up to the deck of the *Samson*, which had come round the north of the island to rescue Vincent, McNeish and McCarthy.³⁶ At King Haakon Bay some fragments of the topsides of the boat had been burnt.³⁷ Evidently it was the Norwegians who understood the boat as a most potent relic and insisted on the *Caird* being brought back; on arrival at Leith Harbour in Stromness Bay, the whalers mustered on the beach and, according to Worsley, they

The *James Caird* on the roof of Selfridges, February, 1920. (**166**)

'would not let us put a hand to her, and every man in the place claimed the honour of helping to haul her up to the wharf'.³⁸ Captain Thom of the *Southern Sky*, the ship that in May 1916 first tried to save the party marooned on Elephant Island, brought the *Caird* to Liverpool on the *S. S. Woodville*, probably as deck cargo, along with a cargo of whale oil for Lever Brothers at Port Sunlight in the hold, arriving on 5 December 1919.³⁹ It was on the *Woodville* that Captain Thom was later to carry Shackleton's coffin from Montevideo to South Georgia for burial in 1922.

The *Daily Telegraph* of 26 December 1919 ('Famous Boat in London') reported that the *Caird* would be exhibited to the audiences at the Albert Hall when Shackleton lectured on the expedition to raise money for the Middlesex Hospital:

> For some time past this boat, now in a dilapidated condition, has reposed peacefully in the Birkenhead shipyard of Messrs. Grayson's, and at the beginning of the week it was

The *James Caird* at the Middlesex Hospital, December 1919. (**165**)

The children of John Quiller Rowett and the *James Caird* at Ely Place, c. 1922. (**164**)

carefully packed up and sent to London... The boat was brought back to London as the only relic of the *Endurance*, and... has lain unobtrusively in the shipyard. Many times it has come near to being broken up, the space it occupied being wanted for other purposes, but it is gratifying to know that every care will now be taken to preserve this relic of a remarkable journey.

In the event the boat was shown on a lorry outside the Albert Hall, as it would not fit through the doors. It appeared also in the garden of the Middlesex Hospital to raise money for their appeal, and on 14 February 1920 as a publicity stunt at Selfridges in Oxford Street it was hauled up the main elevation to the roof garden. In John Quiller Rowett's possession in 1921 – according to Worsley a gift from Shackleton – the boat was kept in the garden at Ely Place, Frant, and the current exhibition shows a picture of Rowett's children at play inside it. Rowett presented it to Dulwich College in March 1922, along with a sledge. The College built a special memorial housing of brick and wrought iron designed by F. Danby Smith; it was open to the elements on two sides. The *Caird* was placed here on 11 April 1924. The boat lived here, apart from an appearance at the British Polar Exhibition at Central Hall, Westminster, in July 1930. The memorial structure was destroyed in July 1944 by a V1 bomb, but the boat was unscathed. The boat was on loan to the National Maritime Museum[40] from 1967 to 1986. In 1968 the College Governors were informed that the Museum 'had carried out considerable restoration work on the boat and this included replacing the mast and sails. It was now in fine condition but because of the mast could not be sited as had been intended in the cloister of the new dining hall block'. The Master and the Clerk had seen the boat and recommended that the Governors should allow the boat to remain on permanent loan to the Museum in return for 'a really good model for display at the College'.[41]. The model was placed in a case in the Lower Hall. The boat was returned to Dulwich College in 1986, thanks to the staunch efforts of the then Master, David Emms, Harding Dunnett and Margaret Slythe. Harding Dunnett accompanied the boat round the South Circular Road blowing his motor horn. It lay on the margins of the College playing fields until it was installed in 1989 in the North Cloister on a bed of shingle from the landing-beach at the head of 'Caird Inlet' in South Georgia bagged by Duncan Carse on 29 December 1972. This was supplemented with a truck-load of similar rocks from Aberystwyth supplied by the local District Council. The *Caird* has been shown at the *Arktis-Antarktis* exhibition in Bonn in 1997–98, and in the following year at the American Museum of Natural History in New York for the exhibition *The Endurance: Shackleton's Legendary Antarctic Expedition* which transferred in December to the National Geographic Society's headquarters in Washington.

While the present overall appearance of the boat is fairly authentic, bearing in mind the lack of any detailed record of the boat and the many vicissitudes she experienced, including being turned upside down at Peggotty Camp to make a hut, no undue reliance should be placed on the actual positioning of fittings on the boat and particularly on her rigging details.

Notes

1   Alfred Lansing, *Endurance*, (1959), 1999, p. 93, says they pulled for 200 to 300 yards at a time, differing from Shackleton's account.
2   Frank Worsley, *Endurance*, 1931, pp. 24, 50.
3   Ibid., p. 52.
4   Lansing, p. 87.
5   E. H. Shackleton, *South*, p. 130.
6   Op. cit., I, pp. 240–241.
7   Frank Worsley, *Shackleton's Boat Journey*, n.d., pp. 12–13.
8   Roland Huntford, *Shackleton*, 1985, p. 469.
9   H. R. Mill, *The Life of Sir Ernest Shackleton*, 1923, p. 198.
10 Worsley, *Endurance*, p. 89; McNeish diary quoted by Caroline Alexander, *The Endurance*, 1998, p. 106.
11 Worsley, *Endurance*, p. 88.
12 Copy in Fisher papers, SPRI.
13 *South*, p. 135.
14 *Shackleton's Boat Journey*, p. 14.
15 Lansing, p. 74.
16 Huntford, p. 462.
17 30 December 1915. Dartmouth College Library, New Hampshire, Special Collections, Ms. Stef. MSS/185, p. 364.
18 *South* pp. 159–160.
19 Huntford, p. 525.
20 Worsley, *Endurance*, p. 89.
21 Quoted by Caroline Alexander, p. 135.
22 Worsley, *Endurance*, p. 89.
23 Orde-Lees. Ts. p. 15, at back of Ms. Diary, Dartmouth College Library, Hanover, New Hampshire. Special Collections, Ms. Stef. MSS/185.
24 Huntford, p. 557.
25 *Shackleton's Boat Journey*, p. 63.
26 Harding Dunnett, *Shackleton's Boat*, 1996, p. 49.
27 Worsley, *Endurance*, p. 91.
28 Leif Mills, *Frank Wild*, 1999, p. 93.
29 Ibid., p. 251.
30 Huntford, p. 186.
31 Ibid., p. 224.

32 Worsley, *Endurance*, p. 105.

33 Ibid., p. 109.

34 Ibid., pp. 122–123.

35 Ibid., pp. 138, 142. Cf. *Shackleton's Boat Journey*, pp. 125, 128.

36 *South*, p. 209.

37 *South*, p. 188.

38 Worsley, *Endurance*, p. 166.

39 Dunnett, p. 83.

40 In turn at the Neptune Hall, the Polar Gallery and the Half-Deck.

41 *Dulwich College Governors' Board Minutes*, 18 October 1968, p. 82.

2 An original sail of the *James Caird*

Canvas

Foot: 170; leech edge: 260; gaff edge: 150; luff edge: 200. Hand-stitched in two vertical lines and at seams

Dulwich College

Probably the Mizzen Lug Sail, part originally of the main sail of the *Stancomb-Wills* (see essay above). Frayed and lacking cringles.

For the making and stitching of the sails on Elephant Island see the entry on the *James Caird* above. It appears that the sails were brought back by the *Samson* from King Haakon Bay along with the boat. The sails had been hung inside the icicles of the cave discovered by Tom Crean, in which they first slept on arrival to screen them from the wind (Worsley, *Shackleton's Boat Journey*, p. 114). Both sails are shown rolled up in early photographs of the Shackleton Memorial at Dulwich with a sign saying 'Actual Sails and Gear used by

Rescue Party on the Journey South Georgia'. This sail has been stored rolled up inside the boat; the larger sail shown in an early photograph of the Shackleton Memorial at Dulwich rolled up alongside this smaller sail appears to have gone missing.

3 NORMAN WILKINSON (1878–1971)
'An Epic of the Sea': Shackleton's Gallant Boat Journey to Seek Aid for his Companions beleaguered on Elephant Island
Exhibited R.A., 1925. Signed (r.h. lower corner)
Oil on canvas. 137 x 188 cm
Dulwich College

Bought anon, 3 July 1925, for £200 (Norman Wilkinson, Account Book), and presented anonymously through Messrs. Stanley Attenborough & Co., Solicitors (*Dulwich College Governors' Minutes, 1925*, p. 40). The Royal Academy did not record the names of the purchasers of paintings until the Second World War.

Norman Wilkinson was a specialist marine painter with much practical experience and observation of the sea and ships. He was a Lieutenant-Commander in the R.N.V.R., and Marine Painter to the Royal Yacht Squadron. He was an expert in camouflage and the originator of the 'Dazzle' painting adopted by all the allied nations in the 1914–18 war to protect merchant vessels against submarine attack. He presented fifty-four paintings of the War at Sea to the nation after the second world war, which are at the National Maritime Museum.

Norman Wilkinson painted three versions of this episode. A smaller (unlocated) canvas *The Voyage of the James Caird* was exhibited at the Royal West of England Academy in October 1924; according to the *Bristol Times and Mirror* (31 October 1924) this was 'one of Mr. Wilkinson's best pictures' for its 'towering waves' and 'luminous skies' above them. 'A cold weary waste of waters reflecting the cold mask of the fast-driving clouds overhead, with a little close-reefed boat hurrying along'. In the earlier version the boat has the mizzen and foresail set, but the picture at Dulwich College shows the wind in the opposite direction and the boat is driven before the wind with a single sail set. A third version (noted in Wilkinson's Account Book as 'Replica (small) 'Epic of the Sea') was bought by McLean from the artist for £73.15.00 on 1 August 1925.

The source for this painting must be the only published eye-witness account available at the time: Shackleton's own version of the Boat Journey published in *South* (1919). Frank Worsley's more detailed account in *Endurance* was not published until 1931. One can understand how Wilkinson was stirred by Shackleton's account beginning in *South* with the sentences, 'The tale of the next sixteen days is one of supreme strife amid heaving waters. The sub-Antarctic Ocean lived up to its evil reputation' (p. 165). It is tempting to think that Wilkinson was showing in his picture the notorious 'gigantic wave', possibly caused by the overturning of an iceberg, which was like a tidal wave and more than forty feet high. Shackleton mistook the crest of the wave for a line of clear sky. However, the wave is surely not shown as high enough, and the incident actually took place at midnight on the ninth day when Shackleton was on watch: 'During twenty-six years' experience of the ocean in all its moods I had not encountered a wave so gigantic. It was a mighty upheaval of the ocean... We were in a seething chaos of tortured water' (*South*, p. 174).

I am grateful to the painter's son, Rodney Wilkinson, for help with this entry.

26 Shackleton (2nd from left) and Scott (at right) onboard *Discovery*.

Early Years and *Discovery* (1901–3)

The Early Years

Dr. Henry Shackleton, newly qualified from Dublin, settled in 1885 in south-east London in suburban Sydenham at Aberdeen House (now 'St. David's' at 12 West Hill, now Westwood Hill), next to St. Bartholomew's Church and down the road from the Crystal Palace. In Camille Pissarro's painting of 1871, *The Avenue, Sydenham* (National Gallery) the house that is the central focus of the painting, to the left of the Church, is the one that by 1885 had been pulled down for the building of the large house belonging to the Shackletons; Pissarro conveys the leisured affluent atmosphere of the suburb, fashionable as it was at that time, with its many large villas taking advantage of the neighbourhood of the Palace with its splendid entertainments. A photograph of the drawing-room shows the fire-place carved with the Shackleton family arms. Behind the house Dr. Shackleton had a famous rose-garden, and the young Ernest built a switch-back slide from the back wall right across the lawn.

Shackleton had been born of Irish and Yorkshire stock, on 15 February 1874 in Kilkea House, County Kildare. The second child, he grew up among a lively family of eight sisters and a brother, and went to a local preparatory school in Sydenham, Fir Lodge; at the age of twelve in April 1887 he was enrolled at Dulwich College. He often walked to school over the hill with a younger boy, John Quiller Rowett; they helped each other with Greek and German.

A day boy at the College, he did 'very little work', according to his contemporary Owen Burne (letter of 10 May 1922 to H. R. Mill, in the Scott Polar Research Institute) 'and if there was a scrap he was usually in it'. His form positions, usually low, twice however show single untypically high results in Mathematics and in English. Returning to the College as the man of the hour in July 1909 to an enthusiastic audience in Great Hall to give the prizes, he remarked, 'I have never before been so near to the prizes as I have been today'. The Master of the day, Arthur Herman Gilkes, wrote in his diary that the hero 'was much pleased' with the silver rose bowl presented by the Captain of School, and 'spoke nicely' to the boys. It must have been at this

time that he was photographed wearing a cornflower, the Alleynian flower, at the door of the South Block. The same month he witnessed one of Brock's famous pictorial fireworks displays at the Crystal Palace showing himself Furthest South. Returning to the College in February 1910, he gave a lecture to the school on the *Nimrod* expedition, and according to the report in the *Alleynian* presented the College Museum with a collection of Antarctic minerals. He put on a slide of a wilderness of ice and snow, showing small men and tiny sledges, and was silent; when the boys began to shuffle their feet, he said, 'You stuck it for forty-four seconds: we stuck it for five weeks'. (S. Hodges, *God's Gift*, p.81) In an article of 1910 ('How I Began') in the boys' magazine, *The Captain*, he says that for all the good points of Dulwich his first year at sea was a better school; he was particularly critical of his English lessons.

A myth, probably put about by Shackleton himself, seems to have grown up that he ran away to sea. Letters in the College Archives from Emily Shackleton are at pains to tell the truth that his father reluctantly agreed to let him leave school early, from the Modern Lower Fourth at the age of sixteen, to join the mercantile marine in April 1890. He served in the White Star Line and the Shire Line, in which he made several voyages round the world, and then in the Castle Line. His love of adventurous literature is shown by the typescript of his own poem of 1895, 'A Tale of the Sea', and his interest in contemporary literature by his signature of 1899 in his copy of Oscar Wilde's anonymously published *Ballad of Reading Gaol*. A photograph shows the ship on which he learned his ropes, the *Hoghton Tower*. A letter to Nicetas Petrides, who claimed to be his closest friend at Fir Lodge and at the College, describes experiences on his first voyage, including a near drowning when he was pulled from the sea by his hair, and a hurricane. From the *Flintshire* he wrote to his sister Kathleen, the artist.

Shackleton's courtship of his fiancée was a local affair – Emily Mary Dorman (of The Firs, West Hill, and later Lynwood, Lawrie Park Road) was a neighbour from a prosperous solicitor's family in Sydenham, a sister of a Dulwich boy and a friend of Shackleton's sister.

A courtship which involved much reading and quotation ensued. A later love-letter to his 'Sweeteyes' has survived.

As Third Officer on the troopship *Tintagel Castle* taking troops to South Africa during the Boer War Shackleton organised burlesque entertainments, and together with the Ship's Surgeon wrote a shipboard magazine, 'O. H. M. S.'. Although both activities were of course traditional features of both nautical and polar expeditions, they were to form an important element of Shackleton's Antarctic expeditions, and their value in keeping up morale among the possibly doomed men would not have been lost on Shackleton.

4 Dr. Henry Shackleton.
Photograph
Private collection

5 Dr. Henry Shackleton and an unknown child
[? 'Joyce Ayers', n. on verso]
Photograph
Private collection

6 The Drawing-room at Aberdeen House, the Sydenham home of the Shackleton family.
Photograph
Private collection

In this room Shackleton first met his future bride, Emily Mary Dorman.

7 *Form and Class Lists, Dulwich College*, Midsummer 1889 and Christmas 1889.
Printed Pamphlets
Dulwich College

In the first listing shown here Shackleton, though absent from his examinations, has a teacher's pencilled mark indicating (from some 'placing meeting' such as are still held today at the College) that he is to go 'above the line', to be promoted to the upper group for his next form. His closest friends Burne and Petrides (see the introduction above) are firmly at the bottom of the class. That Shackleton was not quite the duffer he is made out to be at school is shown by his position in English History and Literature for his next term, at Christmas 1889 in his last school year, where he came second in a group of eighteen boys. Burne and Petrides were meanwhile repeating their third form year.

8 John Quiller Rowett
Letter to Hugh Robert Mill, 12 May 1922
Copy.
Scott Polar Research Institute, MS 100/96/4; D

Describes walking to school with Shackleton.

9 Photograph of Shackleton at sixteen.
Photograph taken from Hugh Robert Mill, *The Life of Sir Ernest Shackleton*, 1922
Dulwich College

10 *The Hoghton Tower*,
illustrated in Hugh Robert Mill, *The Life of Sir Ernest Shackleton*, 1922
Dulwich College

The square-rigged three-masted clipper on which Shackleton learnt his ropes.

11 Nicetas Petrides
Letter to the Editor, *Daily Telegraph*, 3 April 1923.
Copy
Scott Polar Research Institute, MS 100/91/1; D.

School memories.

12 E. H. Shackleton
Letter to N. Petrides, 3 April 1892
Photocopy of transcript by N. Petrides
SPRI, MS/91/3; D

Describes experiences and perils aboard the *Hoghton Tower* to Valparaiso.

13 E. H. Shackleton
Letter to his sister Kathleen, 1895
On rice-paper
Private collection

About life on board the *Flintshire*.

14 E. H. Shackleton, three-quarter length portrait photograph, date unknown.
By a Mayfair photographer
Dulwich College

15 E. H. Shackleton in Merchant Navy uniform.
Cabinet photograph
Private Collection

If there was a cap, it would be possible to identify whether this photograph dates from Shackleton's service in the White Star, Shire or Union Castle Lines; from his apparent age in the photograph this is probably the latter, and from the days of the Boer War troop-ships.

16 'O. H. M. S.', *an Illustrated Record of the Voyage of S. S. 'Tintagel Castle', Conveying Twelve Hundred Soldiers from Southampton to Cape Town, March 1900. Recorded and Illustrated by W. McLean (Surgeon) and E. H. Shackleton (Third Officer),* London, Simpkin, Marshall, 1900.
2.88 x 1.96
The British Library Board

17 'How I Began. Sir Ernest H. Shackleton',
The Captain, XXIII, April 1910
Private Collection

The illustrations, positioned like heraldic supporters to the heading, wittily balance the architectural outlines of Dulwich College against the almost similar ones of 'an Antarctic iceberg'. The article gives Shackleton's views on his education at Dulwich and at sea, his experiences in winter on a ship rounding Cape Horn, his love of poetry and his attempt to be a journalist. It also quotes a poem written on the *Nimrod* expedition.

18 P. G. Wodehouse
'Huy Day by Day', a Diary written about his internment in Belgium, 1940. (Published in *Performing Flea*, 1953, p. 207)
Typescript with manuscript alterations
Dulwich College

Wodehouse describes his hunger when detained by the Germans in the castle of Huy in Belgium during the Second World War, and refers to a conversation with Shackleton, presumably when they met at an Alleyn Club dinner, about the 'jam-puffs' from the Dulwich Buttery, which 'were such a feature of life at our mutual school', and which the hungry hero Shackleton once, during the Southern Journey with Scott on the *Discovery* expedition, dreamed were flying past him in a blizzard. In his prize-giving address at Dulwich College in 1909 in the Great Hall which was 'festively decorated with flags' in his honour (as reported in the *Alleynian* for October 1909), Shackleton mentions the man who served in the Buttery, Collis, rather more warmly than his teachers. For Shackleton's jam puffs, see his *Discovery* diary for 19 December 1902: he dreamed 'that fine [?five] three-cornered tarts are flying past me upstairs, but I never seem able to stop them' (R. Huntford, *Shackleton*, p. 98), and another hungry passage quoted by M. & J. Fisher, *Shackleton*, (p. 63) from a page headed 'Desire': 'pastry three cornered tarts fresh hot crisp, jam hot inside, a pile of these with a bowl of cream'. See also T. H. Orde-Lees, *Endurance* Diary for 1 September 1915 p. 244 (Dartmouth College Library): [Shackleton has] 'a very sweet tooth. Almost nightly the cook is commissioned to produce for him a jam tart, which he fortunately does very well. Three cornered puffs are Sir Ernest's and the cook's speciality'. Jokes about 'the Chief' and his partiality for these tarts were a feature of the *Nimrod* expedition also. John Murray and George Marston's *Antarctic Days* (1913) includes an anecdote of a member of the crew caught by him taking one from the pantry at night (p. 144).

19 E. H. Shackleton at the Dulwich College Prize Day, July, 1909
Photograph signed by Shackleton
Dulwich College

(See the introduction above). Taken outside the South Block. Shackleton wears a cornflower, said to be Edward Alleyn's favourite flower, traditionally worn on Founder's Day.

20 Arthur Herman Gilkes, Master, Dulwich College, 1885–1914
Diary
Dulwich College

Gilkes describes Shackleton's presenting the prizes in 1909. The future Shakespeare critic, George Wilson Knight, who was a boy in the audience at the time, recalled the 'stalwart figure' of the 'hero of the sea', and had 'photographed on his mind' a memory of Gilkes' arm round Shackleton's shoulder: 'his old College failures had been reversed by a world-wide fame... firmly ratified by the acceptance of his former Master' (Ms. in Dulwich College Archives).

21 E. H. Shackleton
'A Tale of the Sea', February 1895
Later typescript
Private Collection

The text is printed in M. & J. Fisher, *Shackleton*, pp. 496–8. For this early romance of Shackleton's see the essay 'A Man of Action and a Man of Books'.

22 C.3.3 (Oscar Wilde)
The Ballad of Reading Gaol,
Leonard Smithers, 1898, sixth impression.
Inscribed 'E. H. Shackleton 1899'
Private Collection

'Discovery'
Scott's 'National Antarctic Expedition', 1901–3

At the age of twenty-seven, Shackleton left his position as Third Officer of the *Carisbrooke Castle*, another Boer War troop ship, and joined the *Discovery* in the London Docks in July 1901, as Third Mate, enrolled in the British National Antarctic Expedition under Captain Robert Falcon Scott. Sir Clements Markham, President of the Royal Geographical Society, judged Shackleton to be 'a marvel of intelligent energy' and both 'high-principled' and 'exceedingly good-tempered' (R. Huntford, *Shackleton*, p. 34.) Shackleton helped select the expedition library and got together playbooks and costumes for the theatricals and entertainments of which he was officially in charge. *Discovery* was the last great British wooden sailing ship, specially built for the expedition in Dundee, and launched on 21 March 1901. She sailed down the Thames on 31 July; Shackleton had taught his sisters semaphore, and by two handkerchiefs at the Albert Docks he signalled 'Goodbye' and spelled

Opposite: **19** E. H. Shackleton at the Dulwich College Prize Day, July 1909.

their names in turn (R. Huntford, *Shackleton*, p. 40). Gerald M. Burn's painting of *The Departure of the 'Discovery' from Cowes* shows the scene next to the Royal Yacht from which King Edward and Queen Alexandra inspected the ship; the King had commanded their presence. Following Carsten Borchgrevink's British Antarctic Expedition of 1898–1900 in the *Southern Cross*, the *Discovery* reached a haven at the head of McMurdo Sound for the winter, and here Edward Wilson, Shackleton's closest companion, a surgeon and a good artist, drew the panorama of the shore.

This was Shackleton's first sight of Mt. Erebus and the Great Ice Barrier (now called the Ross Ice Shelf) and of what he described as the 'weird white world' beyond. Traversing territory previously inviolate by man was plainly a profound excitement for Shackleton.

He was elected editor of the *South Polar Times*, and with Wilson as the artist set up an office in the hold of *Discovery*. He produced the typewritten magazine afterwards reprinted in facsimile. Shackleton noted in his diary (23 April 1902) that 'it came out after dinner and was greatly praised'.

Shackleton was put in charge of the dogs, and then-was selected by Scott along with Wilson for the Southern Journey intending to conquer the Pole. The three posed for their photograph on setting off; Scott did not wish to take his sledging pennant, because of the weight, but Shackleton and Wilson insisted on taking theirs, and Scott acceded. Setting off, they looked, according to Louis Bernacchi in his diary (2 Nov 1902 SPRI) 'like three Polar knights, with banners flying in the wind', 'a small party but full of grit and determination'. They reached 82.28°S on 30 December 1902.

The party experienced a blizzard, extreme fatigue and hunger, frost-bite and snow-blindness; Shackleton developed alarming symptoms of scurvy from lack of vitamin C, with trouble in his chest, eventually coughing blood. Tension between Scott and Shackleton developed into bitter hostility from Scott and a quarrel. It was felt from the start that Scott, a Royal Navy officer, did not easily take to an outsider such as Shackleton from the Merchant Navy, and he was probably jealous of Shackleton's popularity. Shackleton was 'invalided' home in the relief ship at McMurdo Sound, the *Morning*, and left down-hearted. Scott and Wilson named the inlet at their furthest south the Shackleton Inlet. Shackleton received the silver Polar Medal. Scott presented Shackleton with a silver cigarette box.

Returned to England, Shackleton married Emily Dorman on 9 April 1904.

23 GERALD M. BURN (d. 3 November 1945)
The Departure of the 'Discovery' from Cowes, 6th August, 1901.
Oil on canvas
1224 x 2106. Framed 1652 x 2563
Provenance: Sir Ernest Shackleton, by whom given to Jack Barnato Joel (South African financier and friend of Rosa Chetwynd). Given by his son H. J. Joel (of Childwick Bury, St. Albans) to Dulwich College, February, 1943 (*Governors' Board Minutes*, 26 February 1943, p. 11)
Dulwich College

The Times for 7 August 1901 reported from H. M. Y. *Osborne* that on 5 August 'The King and Queen, accompanied by Princess Victoria, paid a private visit to the Discovery this morning previous to her departure on the Antarctic Expedition'. Two other Royal Yachts, the 'Victoria and Albert' and 'Alberta', were present: Burn shows the 'Victoria and Albert' astern of the *Discovery*. Many schooners and cruisers as well as yachts belonging to the rich and aristocratic were present for the fashionable week of the Regatta of the Royal London Yacht Club, though the atmosphere, owing to Queen Victoria's recent death, was more subdued than usual. The previous day a more detailed report in *The Times* said that the inspection of the *Discovery* was made in Cowes Roads. 'The vessel crossed over from Stokes Bay earlier in the morning, and was moored at one of his Majesty's buoys abreast of the Osborne. Their majesties left the Osborne at half-past 11, and were

received at the gangway by Sir Clements Markham, who presented Commander Scott, who in turn presented the officers of the ship and the scientific staff...' 'The king then walked round the upper deck, examining all the laboratories and taking great interest in the special features of the vessel'. Mr. Mill, 'expert in oceanography' (H. R. Mill, the future biographer of Shackleton) was present. 'During the afternoon the officers went on board the Osborne, where they remained about half-an-hour, and signed their names in the visitors' book...', after which the ship was open to visitors. Burn has shown the royal party on the deck of the *Osborne*, and the boat approaching *Discovery* may be the 'launch with officers on board coming alongside on returning from the Osborne', as described in the newspaper. The King, wearing Admiral's uniform, had been piped aboard.

Discovery was a three-masted barque, square-rigged on fore and main, fore and aft on mizzen. Scott wrote in *The Voyage of the 'Discovery'*, 1905, Vol. I, p. 88: 'In the midst of vessels displaying such delicate beauty of outline, the 'Discovery,' with her black, solid, sombre hull, her short masts, square spars and heavy rigging, formed a striking antithesis, a fit example to point the contrast of "work" and "play" '. *Discovery* had a most distinguished and enduring career, chronicled by Ann Savours in *The Voyages of the Discovery*, 1992. The boat's association with Shackleton almost came full circle when the Shackleton Relief Advisory Committee (set up by the Admiralty when no news came of the explorer and his men) had already had their proposal to despatch *Discovery*, refitted and equipped with dogs, tents, sledges and two years' provisions, to search the shores of the Weddell Sea for the men approved by the government. This was on 19 May 1916, before Shackleton arrived in the Falkland Islands looking for a relief ship. *Discovery* was to be placed at Shackleton's disposal, but under the command of Captain James Fairweather. The ship left Devonport on 10 August 1916, accompanied by two armed trawlers for the first hundred miles. Arrived in Montevideo they found that Shackleton's rescue attempt in the *Yelcho* had been successful. Shackleton is thought to have resented that he was not to be in full command of *Discovery* from Port Stanley, and the Admiralty were perhaps somewhat put out to learn of the rescue from the newspapers and not from Shackleton himself. The *Discovery* turned home with a cargo of grain. Many years later, moored at the Thames near Waterloo Bridge from 1937–54 as a training ship for Sea Scouts she was designated a 'living memorial to Scott, Oates, Shackleton and other heroes of Antarctic exploration'. The *Discovery* since 1986 is to be found at the Victoria Dock, outside Discovery Point, at Dundee in the care of the Dundee Heritage Trust and the Scottish Development Agency.

24 Two contemporary post-cards of *Discovery*, both signed by E. H. Shackleton.
Post-marked 1901
Private Collection

25 Postcard from *Discovery*.
'Links of Empire', Card no. 4 ('Wrench's Series').
Post-marked 'Antarctic Expedition. 1901. Discovery'
National Maritime Museum

Incongruously shows a polar bear (not found in the South).

26 Captain Scott and Shackleton on the deck of *Discovery*, Lyttelton Harbour, 1901
Photograph
Scott Polar Research Institute

Edward Wilson and Shackleton to the left; Scott seventh from left.

27 'Group of Officers and Men', *Discovery*
Illustration in R. F. Scott, *The Voyage of the 'Discovery'*, 1905, Vol. I
Dr Jan Piggott

Shows, among others, Tom Crean, Shackleton and Dr. Wilson.

28 (DR.) EDWARD ADRIAN WILSON
(1872–1912)
Panorama of the mountains bordering the Great Ice Barrier. CXLII 'Mt. Erebus and Terror, from White Island to Cape Mackay', from portfolio of views No. 4 from the National Antarctic Expedition 1901–04, published by the Royal Society of London. Electrostatic copy
Scott Polar Research Institute

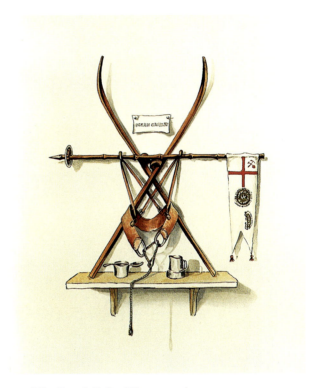

29 *The South Polar Times*, *3 vols*
Reproduced in facsimile by Smith, Elder, 1907
No 1 of the series of 250 copies, most likely (from Markham correspondence found among the pages) the copy of Sir Clements Markham
Queens' College, Harley Street, London, by kind permission of the Principal, Miss Margaret Connell M.A. (Oxon.)

Shackleton was elected editor, and edited the first volume of the magazine before he was invalided home; he typed the magazine, which was illustrated by Edward Wilson. Louis Bernacchi (vol. II) and then Apsley Cherry-Garrard (Vol. III) in turn succeeded Shackleton as editor. Shackleton and Wilson set up an office in the hold of the *Discovery*. Shackleton wrote editorials, and contributed poems. The first number came out on St. George's Day. Shackleton wrote in an article published on his return:

> Our paper, the South Polar Times, which was published in the winter came out once a month, and was contributed to by officers and men alike. I hope to have this published shortly in England. We had a semi-scientific article in every issue, and the lighter side of the expedition was also touched on. The offices of the South Polar Times are situated in one of the food stores, and it was just as impossible to get to the editorial sanctum there as it is to reach the same sanctum of any of the London papers. Dr. Wilson's beautiful illustrations are the feature of the book, and Captain Scott's articles, both humorous and serious, are of great interest. ('Life in the Antarctic', *Pearson's Magazine*, 1903, p. 316)

30 Sledging Flag of E. H. Shackleton
Silk
80 x 90
Private Collection

Gold and red, in heraldic language 'Or, on a fess gules; three buckles of the field'. 'Sir Clements Markham... decreed that each officer should have a personal flag'

(H. R. Mill, *The Life of Sir Ernest Shackleton*, p. 67). When Scott announced that because of the extra weight they would not fly their flags from the sledges on the Southern Journey to the Pole, Shackleton and Wilson said that in that case they would sew them into their shirts, and Scott gave in (R. Huntford, *Shackleton*, p. 88).

31 'The Southern Party'. Photographic illustration in R. F. Scott, *The Voyage of the 'Discovery'*, 1905, Vol. I
Dr. Jan Piggott

Shackleton's sledging flag (**No. 30**) is clearly seen.

32 E. H. Shackleton
Manuscript of 'L'Envoi'
On National Antarctic Expedition headed writing-paper. At end is written 'December 1902. Last rhyme in *South Polar Times*, written on the Southern Sledging Journey'
2 pp
Private Collection

Describes among other things, the sense impressions of sledging. The text is printed in M. & J. Fisher, *Shackleton*, pp. 500–01.

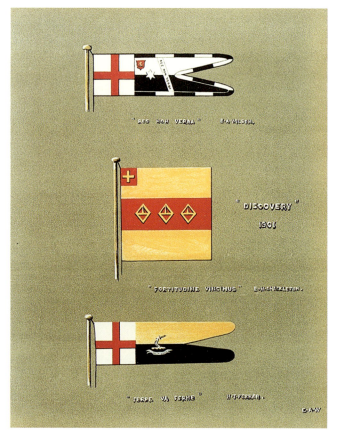

33 E. H. Shackleton
Letter to an unnamed correspondent intending an expedition to the North Pole, 26 September 1903
On mourning writing-paper of the Royal Societies Club, St. James's Street, London. 4 pp
Dulwich College

Offers advice and practical help, without payment. There is no obvious candidate for the addressee of this letter; in 1903 six whaling vessels went to the Arctic from Dundee, and one from Peterhead, but there does not seem to have been an attempt to the Pole. This was quite clearly from Shackleton's letter an English project. Often projected or planned expeditions never took place. (I am grateful for Anne Shirley's help with this note).

34 A silver Cigarette Box, maker's mark 'J. B', retailer's stamp Dobson of Piccadilly. London, 1904.
Rectangular of convex form, with hinged lid, engraved with the 'Discovery Antarctic Expedition, 1901' logo on a belt surrounding a penguin above 'E. H. SHACKLETON/ IN REMEMBRANCE 1901–4. R. F. SCOTT [facsimile signature], cedarwood lining to base, with silver gilt interior to the lid, marked on base and lid.
20.3 x 10.8 x 7.6
The Earl of Portsmouth

32

38

35 Emily Mary Dorman
Photograph
Private Collection

36 E. H. Shackleton
Letter to 'Sweeteyes' (Emily Dorman), from
Edinburgh, n.d., (c. 1904)
Private collection

A love-letter, and also about domestic arrangements.

37 Marriage Service of Ernest Henry Shackleton
and Emily Mary Dorman, 9 April 1904, at
Christchurch, Westminster
Private Collection

38 Emily Mary Shackleton. Bridal Photograph,
1904
Private Collection

Princess Victoria.   The Queen.   The King.

THE KING'S INTEREST IN SOUTH POLAR EXPLORATION: HIS MAJESTY VISITING THE "NIMROD" AT COWES.

DRAWN BY A. FORESTIER, OUR SPECIAL ARTIST AT COWES.

On August 4, his Majesty, accompanied by the Queen and Princess Victoria, visited the "Nimrod," which has been fitted out for Antarctic exploration by Lieutenant Shackleton, and is commanded by Captain England. His Majesty was greatly interested in all the equipment for the expedition, especially in the sledges with which the party is to attempt to reach the South Pole. These are to be driven by motors specially adapted for ice.

Nimrod

The British Antarctic Expedition, 1907–9

Returned from Antarctica, Shackleton took a post in Edinburgh as Secretary of the Royal Scottish Geographical Society; he later stood as Liberal-Unionist candidate for Dundee. However, he now longed to lead an Antarctic expedition.

In August 1907 Shackleton left London as Commander of an expedition which included Frank Wild, Douglas Mawson, Eric Marshall, Jameson Adams, Raymond Priestley, George Marston and Sir Philip Brocklehurst on a converted Arctic sealing schooner, the *Nimrod*. The Norwegian ship was more than forty years old, stank of putrefying seal-oil when first acquired by Shackleton, was inadequate for the amount of stores they wished to carry, could not hold enough coal to reach Antarctica, but was built of teak with immensely thick sides. *The Daily Graphic* commented, based on interviewing John King Davis, her Captain, that 'if the ice catch her there it will lift, not crush her'. Shackleton had her cleaned and converted into an barquentine yacht with three new masts and auxiliary engines. She left from the Blackwall Basin, East India Dock. Shackleton thought of renaming her *Endurance*, after his family motto – *Fortitudine Vincimus*. The ship was commanded to Cowes where the King and Queen Alexandra presented the expedition with flags. The ship left Lyttelton harbour in New Zealand on 1 January 1908, and was towed for the greater part of the journey by the *Koonya*. In the Ross Sea, in spite of a promise which Scott had asked him to make, circumstances forced him to occupy Scott's former winter headquarters at Cape Royds on Ross Island. The expedition took with them a modified Arrol-Johnston motor car, a gift from Sir William Beardmore (which was useless in the snow), ten Manchurian ponies and nine sledge-dogs, but on the dash South they had to rely mostly on man-hauling. They also carried sheep on board.

On the dash south for the Pole, leaving on 28 October 1908, Shackleton, Frank Wild, Adams and Marshall reached Lat 88° 23'S, Long. 162°E. Shackleton showed prudence in his heroic failure by turning back when so near to the Pole; he correctly calculated that he had barely enough rations and fuel to return. He famously remarked to his wife that he thought she would rather have a live donkey than a dead lion. Shackleton had planned his men's diet carefully to avoid the risk of scurvy after his bitter experiences on the *Discovery* expedition. Crossing the Ross Ice Shelf and the Beardmore Glacier, the Southern party faced crevasses, blizzards and near starvation, and showed superhuman endurance; they were out for 126 days, and covered 1260 miles. There were two other sledging parties on the expedition, one to the magnetic South Pole and the other when the summit and crater of Mount Erebus were climbed for the first time and surveyed. Important scientific research was carried out. Recalling this expedition in *South* ten years later, Shackleton wrote of 'high adventure, strenuous days, lonely nights, unique experiences, and above all, records of unflinching determination, supreme loyalty, and generous self-sacrifice on the part of my men' (p. vii).

The story gripped the public imagination on his return to England with no loss of life; this was endorsed by the success of Shackleton's book about the expedition, *The Heart of the Antarctic* (1909). 'Lieutenant Shackleton' was lionised, sculpted and painted, made a Commander of the Victorian Order (the sovereign's personal award) and knighted. Edward VII considered the expedition 'the greatest geographical event of his reign' (R. Huntford, *Shackleton*, p. 298). Shackleton lectured across Europe, was given medals by many crowned heads and institutions, and recorded onto an Edison disk the story of the pony Socks falling down a crevasse to its death.

The *Nimrod* was moored at Tower Pier after her return, when an elaborate exhibition in a hall across the road raised £2000 for London hospitals. Her masts had, of course, to be removed to pass under the four bridges. The fruits of the scientific research carried out by the Expedition were on show; Zoological, Geological and Biological displays included Exhibit 45:

Specimens of the life on the sea floor at Cape Royds up to a depth 60 fathoms. Each bottle is labelled with the name of the class to which the specimens belong; in all cases where possible names familiar to the general public have been used. This exhibit will include: Sea-urchins, Starfish, Worms, Polyzoa, Corals, Sea-slugs, Shell-fish and Sea-weeds. (Catalogue, p. 11)

Sledges and Shackleton's own man-hauling harness from the expedition, the apparatus of endurance, are potent relics. Queen Alexandra's miniature is a token of the special affection in which he was held by her. There are records of the daily life of the expedition and entertainments to be found in diaries, the *Midwinter Celebration at Cape Royds, June 23rd., 1908* Menu and Frank Wild's birthday menu designed by George Marston. One astonishing ruse of Shackleton's to avoid 'polar ennui' or worse during the Antarctic winter was to ship a printing press, type and paper and to produce with very lightly trained hands a remarkable piece of fine printing, in absurdly difficult conditions: the *Aurora Australis*, of which only 60 to 100 copies were produced. For these George Marston produced superb etched and lithographic illustrations.

Shackleton's love of literature, which played such a large part in his consciousness and conversation, is shown by the copies of Robert Browning's poems from the ship's library and by his later association with the Robert Browning Settlement in Camberwell. The verses from a New Zealand school song (shown here in Emily's handwriting) which were important to him, were presumably taught him by Frank Worsley.

John Murray and George Marston's book of 'Sketches of the homely side of Polar Life by two of Shackleton's Men', *Antarctic Days* (1913), closes with a ringing hope that Shackleton will return to the Antarctic: 'Tarry not too long, Shackleton!' (p. 175).

39 B. KRONSTRAND (early 20th Century)
Ernest Shackleton, bust length
Signed and dated 'B. Kronstrand/07' (upper left)
Oil on canvas
76.2 x 63.5
Provenance: Sir Ernest Shackleton; by descent to Mr. and Mrs. Nicholas Shackleton. Sold at Christie's *Exploration and Travel* Sale, 17 September 1999 [257]
The Earl of Portsmouth

Kronstrand exhibited at the Royal Society of Artists in Birmingham, giving his address as Penzance. A label on the reverse of the stretcher records 'Kronstrand, 2, St. Leonards Studios, St. Leonards Terrace' [Polegate].

The portrait is dated the year of the departure of the *Nimrod*, but the decorations were added later: orders from Denmark, Norway and Russia, the Legion of Honour from France; the Royal Victorian Order and the white strip of the Polar Medal. The latest of these decorations was made in 1910 (St. Anne of Russia).

40 S. Y. Nimrod
Ship's Model
Wood, metal, cloth, thread &c.
60 x 117 x 38
The Science Museum
Provenance: Sir Ernest Shackleton; presented to the Museum by Lady Shackleton, 1929

For *Nimrod*, see the introduction above. Though small, old and dilapidated when he first saw her, once she was refitted Shackleton 'grew really proud of the sturdy little ship' (*The Heart of the Antarctic*, I, p. 16).

41 Lieutenant Shackleton's Nimrod
Postcard
Private collection

42 Summit at Erebus
Postcard
Private collection

43 S. Y. Nimrod in Floe-Ice
Postcard
Private collection

44 GEORGE MARSTON (1882–1940)
Panorama of Ross Sea Mountains
Photograph (life-size)
16.5 x 164
Scott Polar Research Institute

47 and 48

45 ERIC MARSHALL (1879–1963)
British Antarctic Expedition, 1907. Route and Surveys of the Southern Journey Party, 1908–09.
Map, from *The Heart of the Antarctic*, 1909
66 x 39
Dulwich College

46 'Lieut. Shackleton's Antarctic Expedition',
The Geographical Journal, XXXIII, 4, April 1909
Dulwich College

The publication of the Royal Geographical Society.

47 and 48 Sledges from *Nimrod* Expedition
Seasoned ash, American hickory, rawhide and rope
26 x 325 x 60
Dulwich College
Provenance: one of Shackleton's sledges (the darker, No. 49) was most likely presented to the College by Dr. John Quiller Rowett (O.A.) in 1922, together with the *James Caird*. The other, No. 50, was the gift in 1924 of J.& T. Bayley Ltd., of 18, Camomile Street, London E.C., who were 'Packers by Special Appointment to the *Nimrod* expedition

of 1908–9'. The sledge appears unused, though the letter of 17 April 1924 calls it 'used by Sir Ernest Shackleton during his expedition to the South Pole in the years 1907–9'. (*Dulwich College Governors' Minutes*, 1924, p. 21).

The sledges were made by the Norwegian ski-manufacturers L. H. Hagen & Co., of Christiania [Oslo], Norway, who were one of the first mass producers of skis; Shackleton went to Norway twice himself, among other things to order sledges and finnesko (boots made of reindeer fur). He used the sledges from *Discovery* as prototypes.

They were suited to cope with the extreme conditions on the crevassed Beardmore Glacier and the Ross Ice Shelf with its pressure-ridges and sastrugi (windblown ridges in the snow). The sledges were hauled by ponies or dogs, by humans, or by a sail and once by the special motor car, the Arrol-Johnston.

Shackleton records in Volume I, Chapter VIII of *The Heart of the Antarctic* (1909), that the sledges were of a type developed by the Norwegian Fridtjof Nansen (1861–1930), and there is a clear sketch and diagram of the sledges on p. 311, showing the bow and stern. The wooden Nansen sledges have been proved the best for the Antarctic conditions, and a metal variant of these sledges is still in use to this day by the British Antarctic Survey, though some modifications have been made.

Shackleton decided that eleven feet was the ideal length of sledge for man-hauling, twelve feet for sledges pulled by horses and seven feet for those used on short journeys. The sledges were rigid in their uprights and yet would give to uneven surfaces. The uppers were made of seasoned ash, and the runners were made of American hickory, which was not sawn but split following the grain. Shackleton never used metal runners after bad experiences with them in the *Discovery* expedition of 1901. The lashings are made of rawhide. The bearers are an inch square, and rested on uprights covered with leather. The ends carry a bow of wood, which was upturned to cope with unequal surfaces and to prevent the sledge being driven into obstructions of snow and ice. At each end was a bight of alpine rope into which a toggle could easily be put for the sledge harness; two sledges could be towed in line. Straps were riveted into the bearers for speedy and trustworthy fastening of loads. The ideal working weight on the sledge was 650 lbs. For the hauling of the *James Caird* and the other lifeboats, the carpenter Harry McNeish made stronger sledges from wood salvaged from *Endurance*. A plate in Shackleton's *The Heart of the Antarctic*, 1909 (Vol I, facing p. 140) shows men 'preparing a sledge during the winter'.

49 Sledge Harness, Manhaul, of Ernest Shackleton

Cloth and leather
92 long
Private Collection

Orde-Lees writes in his Diary for 31 January 1915 (Dartmouth College Library) describing the hauling of the James Caird and the other life-boats:

> the harness consists of a six inch wide webbing belt and shoulder straps attached to a stout lanyard which is in turn made fast by a 'rolling-hitch' to a long rope or trace. The members of the team are spaced out along the rope at intervals of about six feet and if there are two traces the team makes a 'pig-tail' some 50 or 60 ft. long or well over 100 ft. with the boat and a fourteen man team. It forms a fairly unwieldy caravan when it comes to zig-zagging through broken ice or amongst hummocks. (p. 31).

The harness was also of course most important in saving the life of men fallen into crevasses. See Frank Wild's account of 'hanging by my left arm only, in a horrible chasm' when the horse Socks had disappeared 'into an intense black depth' during the dash for the Pole, in his Diary for 7 December 1908 (L. Mills, *Frank Wild*, p. 85).

50 Shackleton's Compass

6.5 x 20 x 2
Engraved 'Br. Ant. Ex., 1907'
Private Collection

51 Nimrod Rug

Woollen, olive green
With the monogram 'EMS' (i.e. Emily Mary Shackleton) and initials 'B.A.E. 1907.9' in raised satin letters.

143 x 193
Private collection

T. H. Orde-Lees, Diary, 31 January 1915.

50

50

55 Miniature of Queen Alexandra

Tinted photo in glazed brass case with hinged ring.
7.5 x 4.4 x 0.6
Private collection

Alexandra (1844–1925) was the eldest daughter of King Christian IX of Denmark; she was welcomed to the Royal Family in a poem by Tennyson of 1863 as the 'sea-king's daughter from over the sea, Alexandra!' Alexandra was known as the 'Queen Mother' from 1910. She is known to have had a certain *tendresse* for Shackleton, ever since he was presented to her on board *Discovery* at Cowes by Captain Scott, and presented him with a Union Flag, which Shackleton hoped to plant on the Pole, and in which Frank Wild slept after it had been planted on the southernmost point (L. Mills, *Frank Wild*, p.100) and in 1914 the silk painted Royal Banner taken on the *Endurance* expedition (No. 93). Shackleton discovered and named the Queen Alexandra Range of mountains on the dash to the Pole.

53 'Penguins Listening to the Gramophone during the Summer'

E. H. Shackleton, *The Heart of the Antarctic*, 1909, Vol II, facing p. 20
Dulwich College

The seated figure is George Marston, who was in charge of the gramophone, which was presented to the Expedition by the Gramophone Company. An article, 'Musical Penguins' in *The Scotsman* for 19 November 1909, quotes Shackleton saying that 'during their privations

and dangers the gramophone they had with them proved a great solace. In the summer time we brought out the machine to the penguin rookery close to our hut, and hundreds of these queer birds waddled out in line and assumed almost human attitudes. They clearly expressed their astonishment at 'Waltz me around again, Willie', and it is only fair to say that this air seemed to offend some of the older birds, who went away in disgust'. Popular records with the men were 'We parted by the shore', 'I and my true love will never meet again by the bonnie, bonnie banks of Loch Lomond' and the

55

universal favourite and Shackleton's favourite hymn, 'Lead, kindly light' (*The Heart of the Antarctic*, II, p. 83).

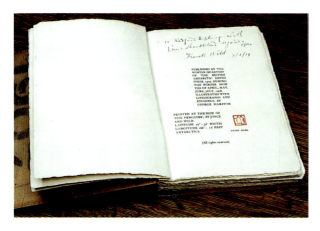

54 E. H. Shackleton, Editor
Aurora Australis
'Published at the winter quarters of the British Antarctic Expedition, during the winter months of April, May, June, July, 1908. Illustrated with lithographs and etchings; by George Marston. Printed at the sign of 'The Penguins'; by Joyce and Wild, Latitude 77°.32' South. Longitude 166°.. 12' East. Antarctica'. 4°.
26 x 19.5
Dulwich College
Lithographed title, eleven lithographed or etched plates by George Marston. The title-page is monochrome, lacking the blue lithograph impression. Original sheep-backed packing-case boards, spine blind-stamped with *Aurora Australis* and imprint of two penguins. Verso of upper cover stencilled 'British Antarctic Expedition 1907'; verso of lower cover stencilled 'Petit Pois'. 'Format A' copy (with illustration of *Nimrod* in dock ('Many Shekels were needed for the ship to go forth') on verso of one unpaginated leaf of 'An Ancient Manuscript'. Presentation copy inscribed and signed by Frank Wild 'To Rudyard Kipling with Ernest Shackleton's regards. 1914', dated 8/6/14. Bookplate of Rudyard Kipling. Letter of June 1942 from Elsie Bambridge about the gift to her father inserted. For Shackleton's admiration for Kipling see entry for the plaque with Kipling's poem 'If' under the *Quest* expedition. Shackleton and Emily were guests of the Kiplings at Bateman's, and it is possible that this volume and the album of Hurley photographs, No 151, were the gift of Mrs. Bambridge to the College, but no evidence has been found.

Midwinter publications were traditional on polar expeditions, Parry's having a weekly newspaper with humorous poetry &c. *The South Polar Times* consisted of one typewritten and hand-illustrated copy, later reproduced in London in facsimile. For the general context of this publication see the last section of the essay above 'A Man of Action and a Man of Books'. Sir Joseph Causton and Sons. Ltd., of London, gave an Albion printing press, a small etching press, rollers, paper and Caslon Old Face type. Ernest Joyce and Frank Wild had only three weeks of instruction at Causton's works, according to Shackleton in the Preface; Marston in *Antarctic Days* says that this was a 'few hours' among 'myriad engagements of exciting days of preparation' (p. 103).

The type-case and the press are to be seen in the photograph of Joyce and Wild's cubicle, known as the 'Rogues' Retreat', facing p. 222 of Vol. I of *The Heart of the Antarctic*. Both Printing Machine (for etchings and lithographs) and Printing Press appear on the ground-plan of 'The Hut at Winter Quarters' on p. 133 of the same volume. Marston and Day's cubicle in which the machine stood off the living-room, is described on p. 145. Marston described the production in *Antarctic Days*:

> It was winter, and dark and cold. The work had to be done, in the intervals of more serious occupations, in a small room occupied by fifteen men, all of them following their own avocations, with whatever of noise, vibration and dirt might be incidental to them. The inevitable state of such a hut, after doing all possible for cleanliness, can be imagined. Fifteen men shut up together, say during a blizzard which lasts a week. Nobody goes out unless on business; everybody who goes out brings in snow on his feet and clothes. Seal-blubber is burned, mixed with coal, for economy, The blubber melts and runs out on the floor; the ordinary unsweepable soil of the place is a rich compost of all filth, cemented with blubber, more nearly resembling the soil of a whaling-station than anything else I know. Dust from the stove fills the air and settles on the paper as it is being printed. If anything falls on the floor it is done for; if somebody jogs the compositor's elbow as he is setting up matter, and upsets the type into the mire, I can only leave the reader to imagine the result (pp. 105–6).

The ink froze, and a candle was set burning below the inking-plate, and the ink then became too fluid. Smuts settled on the paper. Marston used to do most of his printing in the early hours of the morning when it was quiet and still and there was a minimum of dust. Shackleton says that Marston's producing illustrations by etching on aluminium, by 'algraphy', was difficult, as all the water had traces of salt in it which reacted with the

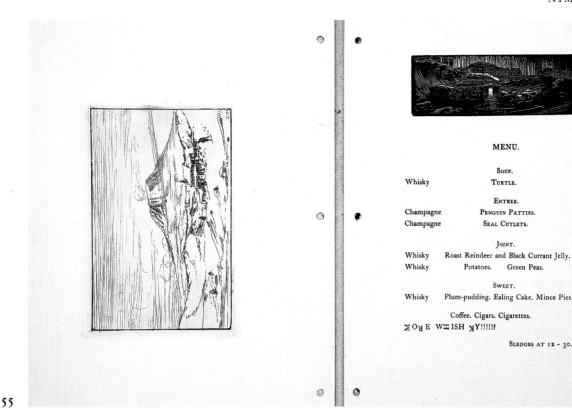

MENU.

| | SOUP. |
| Whisky | TURTLE. |

	ENTREE.
Champagne	PENGUIN PATTIES.
Champagne	SEAL CUTLETS.

	JOINT.
Whisky	Roast Reindeer and Black Currant Jelly.
Whisky	Potatoes. Green Peas.

| | SWEET. |
| Whisky | Plum-pudding. Ealing Cake. Mince Pies. |

Coffee. Cigars. Cigarettes.

ꟺΟꓤE WℲISH ꓬY!!!!!?

SLEDGES AT 12 - 30.

55

sensitive plates (*The Heart of the Antarctic*, I, p. 218). After two or three weeks Wild and Joyce managed to print two pages a day. Then Bernard Day, the motor engineer, bound the pages with green silk cord threaded through punched holes and cleaned, planed, cut, bevelled and polished the boards for the book made from the three-ply Venesta packing cases. Shackleton, who was an expert on stores since his Merchant Navy days, designed these cases, which were 28 x 15 inches. The board was of very thin oak and chestnut with a waterproof cement, and the cases were light, strong and waterproof. (Shackleton in *The Heart of the Antarctic*, I, p. 8, says that birch was also used). 2500 were brought with them, and a feature of the publication was the witty incorporation on the inside of the boards of the stencilled words of the contents, such as J U L I E N N E   S O U P,   S U E T   or   B A C O N, which made copies unique.

55 Menu: 'Midwinter Celebration: at Winter Quarters, Cape Royds. B.A.E. 1907 Lat. 77°..32' S. Long. 166°.. 12' E. June 23rd 1908.'
Printed by the Albion Press, presumably by Wild and Joyce. Etching on left by Marston, woodcut above text. The word 'whiskey' printed as if with alcoholic staggers.
Private collection

'When the shadow of night's eternal wings
Envelopes the gloomy whole
And the mutter of deep-mouth'd thunderings

After a teetotal régime the Midwinter Day, the Great Polar Festival and Birthday festivals were a release, and occasion for a 'wild spree' (*The Heart of the Antarctic*, I. p. 216). The same volume shows a (presumably pre-prandial) photograph of this feast, opp. p. 224, with the room hung with flags. Crackers and champagne, speeches, songs and toasts. On the *Endurance* expedition James's burlesque lecture by a German professor about the calorie and Hurley's stage decorated with bunting were long remembered; on Elephant Island the following Midwinter Day they remembered the 'cocktails' and Veuve Cliquot, having to make do with a tablespoon of methylated spirits in hot water (Shackleton, *South*, p. 234).

56 The Type-case and Albion Press in the cubicle of Joyce and Wild
Photograph
Scott Polar Research Institute

57 George Marston
Birthday Menu for Frank Wild, 18 April 1908
25.8 x 15.5
Black ink with brown ink wash and a touch of gouache
Private collection

Frank Wild was store-keeper

58 *The Antarctic Book*
Winter Quarters, 1907–9
Heinemann 1909. 300 copies were printed, as supplement to the *de luxe* edition of *The Heart of the Antarctic*, and signed by all members of the expedition.
Dulwich College

George Marston's portrait of Frank Wild

59 Frank Wild
Photograph 190 x 130
Private collection

60 A block of twelve Antarctic Stamps with cancel, as used by the B.A.E., 1907
with inscription by E. H. Shackleton, Postmaster, vouching their authenticity, with an envelope addressed to Thornhill Cooper, Esq. of Christ

Church [New Zealand] in Shackleton's handwriting.
New Zealand 1d. Rose Carmine, overprinted with 'King Edward VII Land' in green in two lines
Private collection

These were used on board *Nimrod* and at the Cape Royds base. King Edward VII Land was Shackleton's intended destination, but he landed in Victoria Land owing to the adverse conditions.
Shackleton was appointed Postmaster, and he was sworn in at Christ Church, New Zealand by Sir Joseph Ward in Lyttelton on 21 December 1907 (*Weekly Press*, Christ Church, 8 January 1908). Though the position was unsalaried, he hoped to make 'a quick £20,000 from sales' (R. Huntford, *Shackleton*. p. 312).

61 Robert Browning, *Poetical Works*, Vol. I,
Smith, Elder & Co., 1897
Signature of E. H. Shackleton on recto of frontispiece
M. Ismay collection, National Maritime Museum

57

62 Robert Browning, *Poetical Works,*
two vols. in one, 1906
Presented by Agnes S. Fox to the Officers of the
Nimrod, September 1907, and by Shackleton to
the Robert Browning Settlement, Camberwell,

1 November 1913
The Robert Browning Settlement

A letter inserted from Shackleton says that 'we had it
with us during our stay in the hut under the Polar night'.

63   The Golden Book of the Browning Cross,
    The Robert Browning Settlement
    Signed by Shackleton on distributing the prizes,
    5 July 1909.

The same page records the presentation to him of the
Browning Cross, silver-gilt, with the inscription, 'Sudden the worst turns the best to the brave', from
'Prospice'. Shackleton visited the Robert Browning
Settlement in Camberwell, south-east London, several
times, and became its President in 1914. At the same
visit in 1909 'he hailed the working men as brothers; for
as he told them, he had been a worker ever since he
shovelled coal at Iquique on the deck of his first ship'
(H. R. Mill, *Life of Sir Ernest Shackleton*, p. 163). The Settlement is named after the poet, whose parents taught
Sunday School there, and was an enterprise of the York
Street Chapel 'to relieve the distress of the poor and
needy' in the neighbourhood.

The Settlement is active today, and donations will be
gratefully received by the Warden at Fellowship House,
3 Browning Street, London SE17 1LN.

**64   'Old College Song of Victoria College,
    Wellington, New Zealand'**
    Hand-written and signed by Emily Shackleton, and
    dated 9 August 1917
    On a sheet of pink paper
    National Maritime Museum

A favourite quotation of her husband.

65   'Dawn lands for youth to reap'
    Ms. of poem in Shackleton's hand, dated 27 July
    1917
    On reverse of a post-card with 'Heavenly Twins'
    design
    National Maritime Museum

> *Dawn lands for youth to reap*
> *Dim lands where Empires sleep*
> *And all that dolphined deep*
> *Where the ships swing.*

Marked as '(anon)'; this may well be a composition of
his own.

**66   E. H. Shackleton, Letter to M. C. Christison,
    Secretary of the Alleyn Club**, 14 July 1914. Type-
    written and signed on Imperial Trans-Antarctic
    Expedition writing-paper.
    Dulwich College
    Quotes the lines above, with variant to line l: 'Dawn
    lands for youth to conquer'

67   George Edward Marston and James Murray
    Antarctic Days, 1913
    Private Collection

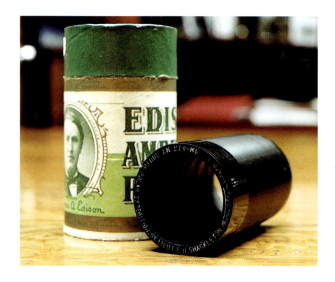

68 E. H. Shackleton

National Phonograph Co. (manufacturers). A wax cylinder record, entitled 'My South Polar Expedition by Lieut. E. H. Shackleton'. Orange, New Jersey, U.S.A. [recorded 30 March 1909]
105 x 55. Contained within original paper-covered cardboard tube, titled 'Edison Amberol Record'
Dulwich College

A four-minute recording summarising the achievements of the expedition and describing the incident with the pony falling down a crevasse.

69 Savage Club House Dinner. Welcome to Lieut. E. H. Shackleton. Capt. R. F. Scott in the Chair, June 19th, 1909. Menu designed by Hassall [sic]; image of *Nimrod* by Charles Dixon

Lithograph, 32 x 37, with signatures
Royal Geographical Society (with the Institute of British Geographers)

Shackleton was accompanied by six of his men to this dinner, at which Capt. R. F. Scott presided. At one point Shackleton whispered to him that Brocklehurst had brought home his amputated frost-bitten toe in a bottle. Scott said that 'before other countries can step in to take the credit of the results of these great works of Mr. Shackleton, this country should come to the fore and organize another expedition (cheers)'. Shackleton replied that he qualified for a savage for eating horse meat raw when there was not enough oil to cook it, and that he agreed with Captain Scott 'that there was more work to be done down South. Never until the British flag flew at the South Pole would the work be accomplished' (unidentified press cutting). According to R. Huntford (*Shackleton*, p.305) Scott said that he was proud to have had a hand 'in rocking Shackleton's Antarctic cradle', at which Shackleton took offence and left immediately after the dinner.

70 **J. A. Stevenson**
    Bust of E. H. Shackleton, 1909
    Plaster, painted, atop inverted globe
    72 x 21 x 38
    Private collection

A bronze version is in the Canterbury Museum, New Zealand.

71 **E. H. Shackleton, Portrait photograph with medals**
    Photographed by Thompson, October 1911
    15 x 11.5
    Signed and dated, April 17, 1918, and with the mount of a photographer in Buenos Aires
    Dulwich College

The Polar Medal and the C.V.O. are to be seen among the many foreign decorations presented to Shackleton on his European tours.

72 **Luncheon Menu at the Berkeley to celebrate Shackleton's Knighthood**, 13 December 1909
    Signed by Marston, Brocklehurst, Shackleton, Mackay, Buckley, Joyce, Davis, Roberts, Armytage and Wild
    17.5 x 23
    Mrs. V. Marston, Hampshire County Record Office, °15AOO/B5

73 **E. H. Shackleton**
    Lecture in German about the *Nimrod* Expedition
    Printed, pp 43
    Private Collection

73 **Harold Begbie, *Shackleton, a Memory*, 1922.**
    Dulwich College

Describes (p. 28) his experiences lecturing in Germany and elsewhere overseas.

75 **The British Antarctic Expedition, 1907–9**
    Pamphlet of 24 pp., printed by Sir Joseph Causton, Ltd., 1909
    Dulwich College

Accompanied the mooring of *Nimrod* at Tower Pier and the adjacent Exhibition of 47 objects, 146 photographs and 40 works by George Marston. £2000 was raised for London hospitals.

76 **'The Nimrod at Temple Pier. Lieut. Shackleton & Lieut. Adams'**
    Post card
    Private collection

Sir Philip Brocklehurst (1887–1975) and *Nimrod*

Sir Philip Lee Brocklehurst, 2nd. Bart., of Swythamley Park, Macclesfield, Cheshire, inherited his title at the age of 17, along with an estate that at the time of his death numbered nearly 4,000 acres. The family's wealth was from banking, mining and silk manufacture as well as in land. After school at Eton he was an undergraduate at Trinity Hall, Cambridge. He took no degree, but boxed lightweight for the University in 1905–6.

On coming down from Cambridge he met Shackleton at a tea-party in Walton Place, Knightsbridge, given by a mutual American friend, Miss Havemeyer. Shackleton asked him, 'What are you doing for the next two years?', to which he replied, 'Nothing much'. And so at the age of 19 in May 1907 he was enrolled in the *Nimrod* expedition. His mother promised financial help. Shackleton wrote to him proposing an elaborate programme of study in geology, surveying and other useful scientific subjects to prepare himself for the expedition.

Included in the sledging-party set to conquer the active volcano Mt. Erebus, he spent his 21st. birthday in a tent at 8750 ft. in a blizzard; for his cake he had one ship's biscuit and a small block of chocolate. He left his three-man sleeping bag, lost a mitt, and in trying to retrieve it he was swept by the blizzard into a ravine. He recovered, however, to venture to within 50 ft. of the crater of Erebus. Because he insisted on wearing his ski-boots rather than *finnesko* (reindeer-skin boots), he became badly frost-bitten. Both his big toes blackened, but he did not give in, and carried his 40lb. pack, which presumably contained his ice-pick and the piece of volcanic rock mined on his birthday, for the two days of the descent. On their return they had a breakfast of champagne, porridge, bacon and eggs. Three weeks later one of his big toes was amputated by Dr. Marshall. Brocklehurst had apparently, along with too many others, been promised a place on the Polar party, but was turned down for having an 'irregular heartbeat' (R. Huntford, *Shackleton*, p. 235) as well as for his frost-bitten toes. As a member of the relief party he had a near escape from being marooned when *Nimrod* was cruising the coast of South Victoria Land looking for him and his two companions who were surveying. Brocklehurst praised Shackleton's solicitude: 'He made

us feel more important than we could have been' (M. & J. Fisher, *Shackleton*, p. 186).

Brocklehurst's name as a member of the expedition is on the printed prospectus for *Endurance*, along with that of his younger brother Courtney, but as Shackleton explains in *South* (p. 340) 'Brocklehurst was to have come South with us, but... as a regular officer, rejoined his unit on the outbreak of war'. (Courtney was also called up). A Lieutenant-Colonel in the First Life Guards from 1914–17, he was wounded. With Shackleton in the North Russian campaign in 1918, he was next a member of the Egyptian Army until 1920. For his honeymoon he motored across the Sahara from Algeria to Nairobi taking two white-topped Chevrolets. In the Second World War Brocklehurst commanded the Second Regiment of the Arab Legion Desert Mechanised Brigade from 1941–2.

77 Louis[e] Johnson Jones (1856– ?)
Sir Philip Brocklehurst and Lieut. Shackleton in the Antarctic
Oil on canvas. Signed 'Louis Johnson Jones'
135 X 72
Johnny and Sarah Van Haeften

Louise Johnson Jones was a specialist in animal paintings. Born at Holywell, Wales, she studied in London, and had three exhibitions at Colnaghi's. In 1907–10 she was carrying out murals at Holywell. At Cheadle Royal she painted a frieze of horses in a landscape. She seems to have been a family friend and visitor of the Brocklehursts, and appears in a snapshot in a photograph album.

Brocklehurst would appear to have shown the artist the photograph he took himself on 3 November 1908, which was reproduced facing vol. I, p. 266, in *The Heart of the Antarctic*, titled by Shackleton 'The Start from the Ice-edge south of Hut Point', which shows Shackleton and the Polar party setting out with the four horses and the dogs; the photograph already had the frieze-like deployment of figures, animals, sledges, flags and heraldic pennants. Queen Alexandra's Union Jack is clearly seen.

The painting shows the four surviving Manchurian ponies from Tientsin out of the ten that the expedition had set out with: the mischievous Quan, Chinaman, the small Socks and the dapple-grey Grisi, who was the best-looking but highly strung. The survivors were white or light-coloured, Shackleton noted (*The Heart of the Antarctic*, I, 161). Bringing the horses on the expedition was not thought to be a success; on the journey south the last remaining pony, Socks, fell to its death down a crevasse.

78 Sledging Flag of Sir Philip Brocklehurst, 2nd. Bart
Silk
66 x 66
Johnny and Sarah Van Haeften
Heraldically: 'Per pale argent and sable three chevronels engrailed between as many brocks all countercharged'. [silver; black; wavy lines; badgers]. The Red Hand indicates an Ulster baronetcy. The coat of arms puns ('canting arms') on the name Brocklehurst and 'brock', an old word for a badger. (Burke's *Peerage, Baronetage and Knightage*, 1927). The flag is shown in the painting above, as is Shackleton's. For sledging flags, see entry for no. 30 above.

79 E. H. Shackleton
Letter to Sir Philip Brocklehurst, n.d., ?1907, 'Instructions for Sir Philip Brocklehurst'
British Antarctic Expedition 1907 writing-paper: 9, Regent Street, Waterloo Place
Johnny and Sarah Van Haeften

Practical surveying, Field Geology (sedimentary, volcanic and igneous rocks).

80 Sir Philip Brocklehurst, Photographed on *Nimrod*
Johnny and Sarah Van Haeften

81 Sir Philip Brocklehurst, Photographed in Antarctic gear
Johnny and Sarah Van Haeften

82 Ice-axe and fragment of volcanic rock from Mount Erebus
Axe: 104 x 31
Johnny and Sarah Van Haeften

The fragment was reputedly broken off with the axe on his twenty-first birthday. For the geological findings see the essay in *Aurora Australis* by Prof. T. W. Edgeworth David, 'The Ascent of Mount Erebus'.

83 Sir Philip Brocklehurst's Snow Goggles from the *Nimrod* Expedition
Leather and brown glass; thin cord ties
Johnny and Sarah Van Haeften

Wearing goggles is essential against snow-blindness. See *The Heart of the Antarctic*, I, p. 273 (n.), and p. 280.

**84 George Marston,
The 'Nimrod'**
Watercolour, with pencil
13.5 x 26
Johnny and Sarah Van Haeften

The watercolour belonged to Sir Philip Brocklehurst. It is based on the ship and setting in the coloured illustration published in *The Heart of the Antarctic*, Vol. I, facing p. 124. Marston made a model of *Nimrod* for Brocklehurst and they kept in touch after the expedition; there are four letters from Brocklehurst to Marston in the Marston papers deposited at the Hampshire County Record Office, 1500/74, 99, 112 and 113. The letters, dated from 1912 to 1923, are from Lapland, Swythamley and East Africa.

85 Sledging Biscuit from the *Nimrod* Expedition
inscribed ' This biscuit was a part of the food the men had who were out in the Nimrod in 1907 with Sir Ernest Shackleton & Sir Philip Brocklehurst in Search of the "South Pole" 1907 and 1909'
Apparently sent with a Christmas card in 1908

from Sir Philip Brocklehurst to Mrs. G. Clarke of Sutton on Sea, Lincs. These biscuits were fortified with 'Plasmon', a concentrated milk protein
Sold at Christie's *Exploration and Travel* Sale, 18 April 2000, no. 152
Johnny and Sarah Van Haeften

Shackleton wrote in *The Heart of the Antarctic* about the dwindling rations on the Southern Party to the Pole, 'We will have one biscuit in the morning, three at midday, and two at night' (Vol. I, p. 336). Wild wrote in his diary for 31 January 1909, 'Shackleton privately forced upon me his one breakfast biscuit, and would have given me another tonight had I allowed him. I do not suppose that anyone else in the world can thoroughly realise how much generosity and sympathy was shown by this; I DO and by GOD I shall never forget it. Thousands of pounds would not have bought that one biscuit' (L. Mills, *Frank Wild*, p. 108). Shackleton did not record the incident in his diary. Later on the return journey the biscuit supply ran out, and they were close to starvation.

86 and 87 The Brocklehurst *Nimrod* photograph albums
Johnny and Sarah Van Haeften

88 Sir Philip Brocklehurst
Letter to 'My dear Panky', from *Nimrod*, Antarctica, 7 Feb 1909
3 pages on B.A.E. 1907 writing-paper
Johnny and Sarah Van Haeften

'Panky' is Baron F.I. Van Haeften, who married Philip's sister Mabel in October 1905. Describes anxieties connected with the return of the two sledge parties, one from the Magnetic Pole and the other the Southern Party; written on board returning to Cape Royds, hoping to find Shackleton. Impatience to return to New Zealand.

156 v *Endurance* at night (detail).

Overleaf:
156 s Ernest Shackleton leaning over the rails of *Endurance*.

Endurance

The Imperial Trans-Antarctic Expedition, 1914–16

The *Endurance* expedition lies at the heart of the Shackleton legend; the pity and terror of the story return an echo in almost every bosom that knows it. The story is best read first in the synoptic narratives of Shackleton in *South* (1919) and Worsley in *Endurance* (1931); Hurley's *Argonauts of the South* (1925) and Hussey's *South with Shackleton* (1949) (also of course synoptic) contain further details, and are both very well written. The details of the men's physical and mental anguish during the Expedition resemble the more excruciating passages of Dante's *Inferno* ; it is from Lucifer after all, where he fell from Heaven, that the eternal ice is said to have emanated. It is in the Ninth Circle, the region of thick-ribbed ice resembling Antarctica, furthest from light and warmth, that Dante places Satan, stogged up to his waist. Uttermost courage in Shackleton's endurance of nature at her most demonic or maniacally destructive; the necessitous three who crossed South Georgia and accosted Mr. Sørlle; the incredulous joy of salvation at Elephant Island and the cry of 'All Well!' from the beach returned to the Boss's enquiry from the boat; the word 'Saved' in Shackleton's handwriting below Hurley's photograph of the boat approaching the island and the waving men (even though Hurley faked the photograph): these details are profoundly moving. Objects salvaged from Elephant Island carry, numinously, the quality of holy relics, and the details of the story become almost a holy writ.

The image of Shackleton in the *Daily Mirror* about to depart for the Pole, caught by the newspaper photographer's camera casually in Oxford Street, implies the extraordinary latent in the ordinary. The narrative changes: the grandiloquent *Prospectus* with the intention 'to cross the Antarctic from sea to sea, securing for the British flag the honour of being the first carried across the South Polar Continent' and the royal send-off is followed by dire necessities; the silk flag becomes something warm to preserve life in sleep. The list of delicacies in the Fortnum's invoice for the provisioning of S. Y. *Endurance*, the meals of blubber and limpet on Elephant Island. George Marston's *Penny Cookery Book*. The beauty of Hurley's images of disaster, resembling

the Ancient Mariner's ship encrusted with rime. (The crew had a copy of the poem which they took with them on the ice after the sinking of the ship). The laconic nobility of Wild's factual memorandum about the expeditions. The pitiful failure to receive the expected monthly radio messages from the Falklands. Relics and photographs of two of the most cheerful of the crew, Leonard Hussey and Charlie Green, are in the exhibition, and also How's affectionate model of the *Endurance*.

Orde-Lees records in his diary that the ship sank bow first, with the stern raised up in the air: 'This evening we were mostly taking it easy and reading. We heard Sir E. call out 'She's going'. It gave us a sickening sensation to see it, for mastless and useless as she has

93

150 n George Marston, *The Landing on Elephant Island*.

been she yet formed a welcome landmark and has always seemed to link us with civilization. Without her our destitution seems more emphasised, our isolation more complete'. (21 November 1915. p. 325. Dartmouth College Library). Orde-Lees plays tribute to Shackleton's superhuman resilience and good humour; the dance on the ice when the ship was firmly beset seems to express perfectly his defiance of disaster: 'Sir Ernest and Captain Worsley danced together on the floe – a one step – whilst I sang & whistled 'The Policeman's Holiday'. It was most amusing & not a little incongruous to see the great polar explorer thus gyrating on the ice' (Ibid., 30 April 1915, p. 120). Shackleton's own formula for endurance recorded in his diary, 'Put footstep of courage into stirrup of patience', gives insight into his extraordinary self-discipline. (19 November 1915. SPRI).

Apsley Cherry-Garrard's review of *South* (*The Nation*, 13 December 1919, pp. 396–97) expresses the spirit of a literary person responding to Shackleton's narrative who also had direct experience of Antarctica:

> A picture haunts my mind – of three boats, crammed with frost-bitten, wet, and dreadfully thirsty men who have had no proper sleep for many days and nights. Some of them are comatose, some of them are on the threshold of delirium, or worse. Darkness is coming on, the sea is heavy, it is decided to lie off the cliffs and glaciers of Elephant Island and try and find a landing with the light. Heavy snow

squalls and a cross sea – and both the wind and the sea rising. Many would have tried to get a little rest in preparation for the coming struggle. But Shackleton is afraid the boat made fast to his own may break adrift. She is hidden by the darkness, but a breaking wave reveals her presence every now and then. All night long he sits with his hand on the painter, which grows heavier and heavier with ice as the unseen seas surge by, and as the rope tightens and droops under his hand his thoughts are busy with future plans.

Marooned on Elephant Island, the men for four and a half months on a narrow rock ledge between sheets of ice and a mass of steep rock were subject to 100 mph. winds, snow, revolting food; they looked out towards Cape Wild at solid pack-ice for unlikely relief. When Macklin returned there with the *Quest* expedition, he wrote: 'Elephant Island, the home of all foul winds that blow – what crazy impulse sent me again to these abandoned regions?' (F. Wild, *Shackleton's Last Voyage*, p. 153). They crowded into the Hut like 'semi-frozen sardines' (F. Hurley, *Shackleton's Argonauts*, caption to photograph of the boat-huts). On Midwinter Day, 22 June 1916 a grand concert of twenty-four turns, medical student songs, sea shanties, negro minstrel songs, and a few new topical songs took place, and Wild wrote in his diary, 'so ended one of the happiest days of my life' (L. Mills, *Frank Wild*, p. 252). Relics from desolate Elephant Island must be very few. Hurley's three canisters of film and glass negative plates were put aboard during the

156 ii The Hut on Elephant Island.

156 jj The Hut on Elephant Island (interior by George Marston).

156 hh Frank Hurley outside the Hut.

few minutes loading the boat which took them to the *Yelcho*, but the boat also carried Marston's sketch-book and his satchel, Wordie's volume from Everyman's Library, the pages of the *Encyclopædia Britannica*, and Hussey's flensing knife. The *Penny Cookery Book* (which may or may not be the original copy used on Elephant Island) lacks the grime from soot and blubber on the other paper items from the upturned boat huts, but might of course have been preserved like the sketch-book in Marston's satchel; it is a loan from the Marston family of an old copy of what was obviously the standard family cookery book, and is a particularly poignant relic, the subject of nightly reading and dis-cussion – 'the most popular book in the world with us', according to Hurley (*Argonauts of the South*, p. 264). Orde-Lees wrote one night,

We want to be fed with a large wooden spoon and, like the Korean babies, be patted on the stomach with the back of the spoon so as to get in a little more than would otherwise be the case. In short, we want to be overfed, grossly overfed, yes, very grossly overfed on nothing but porridge and sugar, black currant and apple pudding and cream, cake, milk, eggs, jam, honey and bread and butter until we burst, and we'll shoot the man who offers us meat. We don't want to see or hear of any more meat as long as we live. (Quoted A. Lansing, *Endurance*, p. 200).

A number of the 'topical songs', as the men referred to them, have survived; George Marston's manuscript ballad is a marvellous wry comic narration, perhaps designed to tell the tale if the paper outlived their bodies on that most desolate isle:

> *They sailed there in a ship Sir*
> *A ship made of wood*
> *It was the very strongest ship*
> *That build of wood they could*
>
> *That ship she was so strong Sir*
> *That she would never yield*
> *So when the ice it pressed too hard*
> *She just kicked up her heels*
>
> *Yes she kicked up her heels Sir*
> *And went to Davy Jones*
> *And there she lies on the bottom now*
> *A rotting of her bones*
>
> *Then we looked very glum Sir*
> *As glum as glum could be*
> *A sitting on the cake of ice*
> *In the middle of that sea.*
>
> *Some came from the N Sir*
> *And some came from the S*
> *And some from Hull a place between*
> *Which is neither N nor S.*
>
> *At length the ice broke up Sir*
> *And we were cast ashore*
> *On a desert Isle where*
> *Penguins, seals & Elephants do roar.*
>
> *Then six men in a boat Sir*
> *Left us to find relief*
> *And we were left on shore to pine*
> *Of hunger & of grief.*
>
> *We gave them of our best Sir*
> *Of the best we had gave we*
> *We gave them of the best we had*
> *And the skipper the rest took he*
>
> *The 22 men left Sir*
> *Were a merry company*

They were bright merry men
In fact good company.

And when we came to argue
We never lost our wool
But froze each other with a look
We were so very cool.

And if we saw a seal Sir
We banged him on the head
We cut and ate the whole lot up
Including of his guts.

And if we saw a penguin Sir
We banged him on the head
We cut and ate the whole lot up
That is except the head.

The Kernel* wrung a petrel's neck
A pretty bird to see
And when it flew away he said
There goes my f...... tea.

And if we'd seen a mouse sir
Not twenty mice but one
I think that we would have killed it sir
With pitchfork and with gun.

And we lived there months and months Sir
As happy as could be
Until we started writing topical verse
As topical as could be.

We sung to one another
These songs of topical verse,
We sang to one another until
Each required a hearse.

And when the ship it came in
It found but me alive
And I as you can plainly see
Am only skin and bones.

And when I tell this tale Sir
That I have told to you
I'm haunted by the voices of
That gostly [sic] croaking crew.

* Kernel, i.e. Colonel, one of Orde-Lees' nicknames (A. Lansing,
    Endurance, p. 76).
(Poem printed by kind permission of Mrs. Veronica Marston from
manuscript lodged with Hampshire Record Office, Ms. 15A00/B
10, on display in this exhibition [catalogue **no.150m**]).

Walter How, *Elephant Island* (Dulwich College).

'Another week's delay', wrote Hussey, 'and most of us
would have been dead' (*South with Shackleton*, p. 2). The
conditions of eating were unspeakable, with food cold
before you had eaten half of it from your pannikin;

water covered in ice to drink, and your breakfast water
carefully melted overnight from a few chips of ice in
tobacco tins; 'one has to lie very still all night so as not
to spill it' (*South*, p. 108). A spoon was 'about one's most
precious possession' (Hussey, *South with Shackleton*,
p. 75). On the ice-floes there had been the occasional
luxury of the twenty-eight undigested fish found in the
belly of the sea-leopard which they shot. Now limpets,
seaweed and 'paddies' (the sheathbill, *Caronax Alba*)
for survival. Macklin's diary gives the Elephant Island
menus for three meals a day: for example, penguin
steaks, Trumilk, Seal hoosh, penguin leg and liver
hoosh, fried gentoo liver, biscuit fried in blubber; no

156 kk Skinning penguins.

lunch the day of Blackborow's amputation; sardines hidden by Orde-Lees for his birthday; limpets; 'last issue of nut food' (transcribed by Fisher, Scott Polar Institute). The best account of 'hoosh', intended by Army experts to defy scurvy, is in Worsley's *Shackleton's Boat Journey*, (p. 113):

> A corruption of a North American Indian word 'hooch,' meaning a drink, but now used in the form 'hoosh' for a sloppy food that can be consumed by drinking ... It was composed of lard, oatmeal, beef protein, vegetable protein, salt and sugar... Made up in half-pound bricks for one man's meal, it had the consistency of a new cheese and a yellow-brown colour, but looked, when boiled with water, like thick pea-soup.

The aluminium 'cooker' or pan, a Shackleton family relic later used to feed chickens, fits the description of the pan carried all across South Georgia on the Trek. It had also been used (held by two men while a third party held the Primus, and lifted clear whenever the boat moved violently) on the *Caird*, when moulting reindeer hairs got in their hoosh.' 'Wrapped in one of our blouses' it was 'flung down' the waterfall at almost the very last stage of the Trek (Shackleton, *South*, p. 205). A possible explanation of why the pan was mysteriously kept after the Primus stove itself had been abandoned when they ran out of fuel may be that the name of

Sørlle, probably their main ally on South Georgia, was scratched on the inside of the cooker, and this was perhaps to be a clue laid in case their bodies were found. Several chairs from the Sørlle's villa at Stromness are held to be the one into which Shackleton collapsed; all one can say is that they were part of the Manager's furniture in his parlour.

Meanwhile, on the other side of the continent, a grim corollary to the endurance and ordeals of Shackleton and his crew was being played out by the Ross Sea or *Aurora* party, whose job was to lay supplies for the party crossing the continent, and who are the subject of a recent book, *Shackleton's Forgotten Men* by Leonard Bickel, and many articles in the press. George Marston referred to these men in a lecture of 1923 at Bedales School:

> These men were not going to have much share in the glory if the expedition succeeded; they would never reach the Pole; they were merely making the task possible for others. Yet they persevered in the face of superhuman difficulties, they faced sickness and death, and pushed on when they could no longer walk and barely stagger, they were starved and frozen, one lost his life; but they laid the depots. ('Mr. Marston's Lecture', *Bedales Chronicle*, April 1923, p. 48.)

From Shackleton's return after the expedition we show two examples of his celebrated speaking engagements,

156 n Look-out post with Union Flag.

the recruiting speech in Sydney, Australia, 'Sir Ernest Shackleton's stirring Appeal for Men for the A. I. F.' and a Philharmonia Hall lecture pamphlet.

89 The Queen Mother's Union Flag
Silk, with bamboo pole and commemorative silver plaque, giving dates of the movements of the *Endurance*. Engraved with Ernest Shackleton's signature, and dated 10 August 1917
With pole: 247.2 high x 14.6 wide (furled)
Lent by Her Majesty the Queen. Photo: The Royal Collection © 2000 Her Majesty the Queen

On 5 August 1914 'The King sent for me' (*South*, p. ii). In the course of twenty minutes of conversation the King gave his silk Union Flag to accompany the Expedition. It was returned by Shackleton in May 1917

(H. R. Mill, *Life of Sir Ernest Shackleton*, p. 249); the King's Flag is now in the Royal Library at Windsor Castle, and the Queen Mother's Flag is kept in the Ballroom at Sandringham House. This flag was the gift of the Queen Mother, Alexandra, presented during a 'prolonged visit' on 16 July 1914 on board *Endurance* at the South-West India Dock together with her sister Maria Feodorovna, the Dowager Empress of Russia. She gave the small Union Jack at the same time as her miniature Royal Standard, two Bibles and an enamel medallion of St. Christopher (*Daily Chronicle*, 17 July 1914). Shackleton had left behind the Queen's flag presented at Cowes on *Nimrod* 'like a sentinel amid the solitude of antarctic snows', but now brought back his flags. After the return of the flag to Her Majesty after the *Endurance* expedition a silver commemorative plaque was added.

After the *Endurance* sank Shackleton raised the King's Union Flag, and it is to be seen on the look-out platform in Hurley's photographs. Hussey says (*South with Shackleton*, p. 72): 'The following day Shackleton decided on one of those actions which can mean so much to the morale of a body of men when they are in a tight corner. It was to hoist the Union Jack which had been personally presented to him by King George V at Buckingham Palace. The sight of it floating over the Antarctic desolation cheered us up a lot. It seemed a

splendid gesture of defiance to the ice to see our National flag flying proudly in the breeze'. According to Worsley (*Endurance*, p. 26) Shackleton said to him 'I don't suppose the King thought when we were talking, any more than I did myself, that I should ever find myself in this pickle'. Hoping to raise the Union Jack on Elephant Island when they saw the *Yelcho*, they found it frozen into a solid compact mass, and had to hoist Macklin's jersey instead (*South*, p. 239). On the Southern Journey of the *Nimrod* expedition Worsley slept in the Queen's Union Flag after they had planted it Furthest South.

90   Royal Standard displaying the British Royal Arms as borne by King Edward VII impaling the Arms of Queen Alexandra

Painted silk

104.2 x 201.9

Sold at Christie's *Exploration and Travel* Sale, 17 September 1999, lot 265

Neil M. Silverman

When Queen Alexandra inspected *Discovery* at Cowes in August 1901, she had 'noticed the fine carnations which Dr. Shackleton had sent to decorate his son's cabin' (H. R. Mill, *Life of Sir Ernest Shackleton*, p. 60). Shackleton wrote on the *Nimrod* expedition how in the Hut at Cape Royds the circle of light moved across the King's portrait and found that of Queen Alexandra: 'It seemed an omen of good luck… today we started to

strive and plant Her flag on the last spot of the world that counts as worth the striving for though ungilded [?unguided] by aught but adventure' (*Nimrod* diary, quoted M. & J. Fisher, *Shackleton*, p. 202). When the Queen visited *Endurance* she spent three times as long as intended, according to the article in the *Daily Chronicle* quoted in the above entry, 'not deterred by narrow gangways and steep ladders from exploring every part of the Endurance'. In the saloon she presented her gifts, including this miniature replica of the Royal Standard which was flown over Marlborough House. It is to be seen in Hurley's photograph of the Midwinter Dinner of 22 June, 1915. After her visit she sent a touching telegram of farewell and God-speed.

91   'The Imperial Trans-Antarctic Expedition' (Prospectus)

30 pp., with map of intended crossing of Antarctica and plan in section of *Endurance*

Private collection

92   Signatures of the members of the *Endurance* Expedition

2 sides, on *S. Y. Endurance* writing-paper

Private collection

Dr. Macklin signs himself as 'carbonero' and Orde-Lees ' as chauffeur', referring to stoking coal and Orde-Lees being 'an expert on all motor matters' (*Prospectus*). The signatures include Sir Daniel Gooch, Bart.

('dawgs') who had sailed as far as South Georgia to help tend the dogs, but then turned home. This (incomplete) list of signatures must therefore date from before 5 December 1914.

93 'Unknown in London: Shackleton pauses on his way to the South Pole'
The Daily Mirror, front page, 31 December 1913
Press-cuttings book
Private Collection

The newspaper comments that Shackleton by the kerb in Oxford Street was 'lost in a "brown study"', and the only man not to be wearing an overcoat.

94 Messrs Fortnum & Mason, Ltd., Invoice of 'valued order consisting of 7 cases delivered yesterday to the S. Y. 'Endurance''.
Two pages, with covering letter, dated 30 July 1914.
Private collection

These items are luxurious foods in small quantities that must have been for special occasions, such as birthdays or Midwinter celebrations, for example 'Carlsbad Plums in Brandy', 'Game Paté Truffles', 'Sugar Almonds', 'Mint Bulls Eyes'.

95 HB Club Farewell Dinner Menu, 31 March 1914, Oddenino's Imperial Restaurant
Design by W. H. (Walter How), with signatures of Shackleton, Marston and Wild
23 x 18.5
Dulwich College

Cartoon figures of Wild and Shackleton, of plump 'Putty' Marston with pipe, and Orde-Lees in an aeroplane.

96 *Endurance* newly arrived at South West India Dock
News Photograph
Private collection

Before she was painted black, and showing one of the lifeboats.

97 Queen Alexandra, the Queen Mother, and her sister Maria Feodorovna, Dowager Empress of Russia, with Lady Shackleton on board *Endurance*, 16 July 1914
Photograph
Private collection

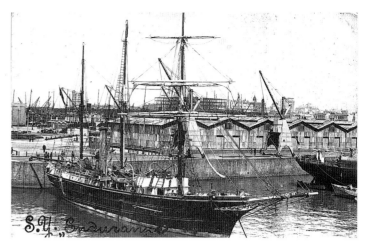

98 *S. Y. Endurance* at Buenos Aires, October 1914
Post-card
Dulwich College

En route for South Georgia and the Antarctic. The ship had leaked on the voyage out, some of the crew had been difficult, and the supply of stores was proving a problem.

99 Frank Hurley
Photograph 'The Boss' (Shackleton)
Signed by Shackleton
Private collection

Shackleton is wearing the man-haul sledge harness (see No. 49).

100 Frank Hurley
Signed photograph of the crew of the beset *Endurance* (copy)
Scott Polar Research Institute

There is a filmed version of this group photograph being assembled in Hurley's *South*.

101 South Polar Chart,
No. 1240. Hydrographic Office, 1956
67 x 102
Marked in black and brown marker pen and Letraset with routes of the *Endurance* and *James Caird*, and showing the Ross Sea (*Aurora*) routes.
Dulwich College

102 Walter How
Model of *Endurance*
43 x 60, in frame 51 x 70
Scott Polar Research Institute. Gift of descendants of Walter How, 1996.

102

Walter How (A. B. on *Endurance*) made many sketches of Shackleton's expeditions, from memory and other sources; some of these ('from his sketch-book') were used as vignettes in M. & J. Fisher, *Shackleton*, 1957. The authors had the benefit of his reminiscences; he died in 1972 at the age of eighty-seven. Before How joined *Endurance* he had much experience in sail off the coast of Labrador. Later he became an amateur painter and maker of model ships; many sketches of his survive.

103   Frank Hurley
'The "Endurance" after Winter. 1915.
Pressure Approaching'.
Title inscribed, signed and dated by Shackleton,
September 1917
48.6 x 38
Dulwich College
Once in possession of Sir Raymond Beck, Chairman of Lloyd's of London; presented to the College by T. H. Peace, Esq., M. C. and Bar, O. A., 1916–2000.

104   'Sir Ernest Shackleton's Imperial Trans-Antarctic Expedition, 2nd. Lieut L. D. A. Hussey, R. G. A., Meteorologist to Sir Ernest Shackleton's Antarctic Expedition'.
A pamphlet about Hussey's Banjo, 4 pp., n.d.
Published by the makers of Windsor Banjos and other instruments
22 x 14
Private collection

'But the song of Lost Endeavour that I make,
Is it hidden in the twanging of the strings?'

Kipling, 'The Song of the Banjo' (1894)

With photo of Hussey in uniform performing on the banjo and 'Mr. L. D. A. Hussey's Windsor Zither Banjo (Number 5 Popular Model). Photographed immediately on his return from Sir Ernest Shackleton's Expedition. 9/11/16'. (Showing the case and the few surviving packets of his 'Castle Brand' strings). Shackleton insisted on Hussey retaining his Banjo as a 'vital mental medicine' when the party all had to

156 v The *Endurance* at night.

dispose of unnecessary personal items (Hussey, *South with Shackleton*, p. 65). Shackleton recounts in *South*, p. 12 how the penguins were played 'Tipperary', and appeared to enjoy it, but 'fled in horror from Scottish music'. A charming pen illustration of Hussey playing his banjo to the penguins appears in Hussey's *South with Shackleton*, p. 30. Hurley in *Argonauts of the South*, p. 148, writes appreciatively of Hussey playing the latest London music-hall 'hits' to the penguins from the poop. Letters from Hussey to the makers of the Banjo quoted in the pamphlet say that Shackleton said that it helped to save the lives of the party. The value of the banjo on Elephant Island was well attested by the diaries of the men (See R. Huntford, *Shackleton*, p. 538), and Hussey was called on to accompany the 'topical songs' that they wrote and whose performance kept up their spirits. 'Hussey usually treats us to a half hour's banjo serenade in which our choristers join their voices' (L. Mills, *Frank Wild*, p. 247); the popular tunes

were 'Break the news to Mother', and 'Only a beautiful picture in a beautiful golden frame'. The banjo (today in the possession of the National Maritime Museum) has on the vellum the signatures of all the members of the expedition. Referring to the banjo as his 'Jo', Hussey says that he had it with him in Central Africa just before he joined *Endurance*, and that 'Next time I go South I shall certainly take a New Windsor with me'. Hussey was indeed a member of the *Quest* expedition. It was he who after the interment of Shackleton placed bronze wreaths in the church at Grytviken, one from King George V and the British people, the other from his old school-fellows resident in South America' (F. Wild, *Shackleton's Last Voyage*, p. 194).

105 Leonard Hussey in uniform, wearing the white stripe of the Polar Medal,
c. 1917
Studio photograph
27.5 x 20
Private collection

Commissioned on his return, Hussey joined Shackleton in North Russia on Operation Syren.

106 Hussey's Pannikin from *Endurance*
18 x 10
Aluminium
Private Collection

The pannikins (or 'pannicans', according to A. Lansing,

Endurance, p. 69; sometimes 'sledging-mugs', according to Shackleton, e.g. *South*, p. 89) used on the *Endurance* expedition were of the same type as those seen in the vignette of skis in *The South Polar Times* (see p. 67), and thus derive from *Discovery* or earlier. Shackleton describes them in *The Heart of the Antarctic* (I, p. 155) as made of aluminium, in pairs that fitted together (obviously for economy of space): 'the outer panikin, for holding the hot tea or cocoa, was provided with handles, and the other fitted over the top of this, and was used for the more solid food'. Sledging utensils were taken for the shore party alone; when the crew also were forced to leave the ship, this meant that there were not enough sets to go round. Orde-Lees says in his diary (17 December 1915, p. 351, Dartmouth College Library): 'the original set consists of an aluminium jug and a mug for each man. The jug and mug are so constructed that the latter inverted fits over the former the handle of which folds. Thus on Elephant Island, four had mugs, four had jugs'. Three pannikins feature conspicuously in Hurley's photograph of 'The First Meal on Elephant Island and the First Hot Meal for Several Days'. Inside the upturned boat hut, Hurley described how 'extra blubber lamps are lit in the centre of the seated circle, lighting up grimy faces with their smoky flare. It is a weird sight – the light thrown up by the lamps illuminates smoke-grimed faces like stage footlights, and is reflected in sparkling eyes and the glint on the aluminium mugs'. (*Argonauts of the South*, p. 262).

107 Hussey's Altimeter from *Endurance*
2.2 x 7.5
Private collection

Hussey's official post on the expedition was as meteorologist; on *Quest* he served as meteorologist and assistant surgeon.

108 Dr. L. D. A. Hussey, O.B.E., (1894–1965)
South with Shackleton, 1949
Illustration of Hussey, banjo and penguins by Victor J. Bertoglio, p. 29
Dr. Jan Piggott

Hussey recounts his experiences up to and including his time marooned on Elephant Island, with a later chapter on *Quest* and Shackleton's death. Hussey in early 1914 was in the Sudan, taking part in a dig connected with medical archaeology, and read of Shackleton's proposed *Endurance* expedition in a month-old newspaper. Shackleton interviewed him cursorily, and later told him that he had appointed him because 'I thought you looked funny' (p.5).

109 Charles Green (1888–1974)
Photograph with Autograph
20.3 X 12.7
Private collection

Taken in Buenos Aires just prior to Charlie Green's joining *Endurance* as Cook. The cook of *Endurance* had just been sacked for drunkenness, and Green left his job on the *Andes* to join Shackleton. When asked by Shackleton on the ice-floe what he would do with his pay when he returned home, Green said that he would come on another expedition with him, and he did indeed join the *Quest*. Green said that the worst episode was the boat journey to Elephant Island with the exposure and the presence of the killer whales. Only once, on arrival at Elephant Island, was he noticed to lose his habitual grin. See the privately printed biography by his nephew, Roy Cockram, *The Antarctic Chef*, 1999. [Copies may be ordered in the exhibition bookshop]

110 Charles Green
Hurley's photograph of Green preparing seal meat in the *Endurance* galley
A page from Green's own album inscribed by himself
25.4 X 13.4
Private collection

The white blur alongside Green's left leg is the ship's cat, Mrs. Chippy. 'If chided about the leathery toughness or cinder-like crispness of a seal steak [Green] had a ready fund of wit which always completely exonerated him and laid the blame on the seal' (Hurley, *Argonauts of the South*, p. 204).

111 Charles Green
Hurley's photograph of Green preparing penguin in the *Endurance* galley
18.5 X 13.4
Private collection

112 Charles Green
Hurley's photograph of Green cooking on the blubber stove at 'Mark Time' ('Patience') Camp, January 1916
18.5 X 12.7
Private collection

A 'blubber-stove' was improvised by Hurley at Ocean Camp from the ship's steel ash-chute by punching holes at its top, with an oil-drum on top, and a chimney made from biscuit-tins. On it Green managed to make bannocks or scones on a hot sheet of iron. The wheelhouse from the ship was set up, and with sails and tarpaulins this 'made a very cosy place inside' (Hussey, *South with Shackleton*, p. 76). Shackleton was amused and encouraged to hear the men telling Green whether they liked their tea strong or weak; he told them that the tea would be the same for all hands, and that they would be fortunate if two months later they had any tea at all (*South*, p. 80). At Patience Camp there was a screen made from four oars and an old sail. Shackleton said that Green and his mate looked 'black as two Mohawk Minstrels' (ibid., p. 104). Shackleton praises his 'unflagging energy' in preparing 'savoury and satisfying' meals (p. 155).

113 Charles Green
Brass Compass
2.8 diam
Private collection

Many of the seamen had 'personal' compasses; it is believed that this was used in the open-boat journey to Elephant Island.

114 Charles Green
Medal Ribbon Clasp
1.2 X 12.7
Victory, 1919; Mercantile Marine, 1919; 1914–20 British War Medal; 1914–16 Bronze Polar
Private collection

115 Len Hussey's Sheath Knife
27.5 X 6
Steel, brass, wood, with leather sheath slitted for carrying on a belt
'L. Hussey I.T.A.E. 1914–191 ' [sic]
Private collection

Used to kill, skin and cut up seal and penguin, cut blubber in strips for the fire, scrape snow off the walls of the hut and at meals; brought back from Elephant Island.

116 James Wordie's copy of Young's *Travels in France, during the Years 1787, 1788 1789*, Everyman's Library, 1913, used on Elephant Island.

156 w Patience Camp, kitchen.

With list of occupants of No 5 Tent (Clark, Macklin, Rickinson, Worsley, Kerr, Blackboro, Greenstreet, Wordie) on 27.1.16 (the day after Patience Camp was set up) on fly-leaf. On end-paper a label of the British and Foreign Sailors Society, presenting the book to 'Sir Ernest Shackleton's Antarctic Expedition, 1914'. An undated typewritten signed note by J. M. Wordie, on St. John's College, Cambridge, writing-paper attests that this was with him 'when south on the *Endurance* and on Elephant Island'
Private collection

117 Fragments of *Encyclopædia Britannica* used on Elephant Island by James Wordie.
(Scientific subjects). 11th edition, 1911, india paper
With typed label, 'used as reading material whilst on Elephant Island'
Private collection

Volumes of the Encyclopædia were saved from the wrecked *Endurance* by Hurley from Shackleton's cabin (*Argonauts of the South*, p. 198), 'ultimately being used to settle the inevitable arguments that often arose. Owing to shortage of matches we were unfortunately driven to use the Encyclopædia for purposes other than purely literary ones, though one man discovered that the paper

had been impregnated with saltpetre, thus making it a highly efficient pipe-lighter' (L. Hussey, *South with Shackleton*, p. 78). Hurley rolled cigarettes with 'pages containing articles of inhuman interest' (op. cit., p. 275).

118 The Penny Cookery Book
n.d., 76 pp., lacking title page
Mrs. V. Marston

See introduction above. According to Worsley, (*Endurance*, p. 187) Wild said that the Book was 'sometimes dashed annoying', as it reminded you of 'things we couldn't get'.

119 Frank Hurley
'The Start of the 750 mile Boat Journey'
Title and signature by E. H. Shackleton
13.5 x 19
Dulwich College

120 Frank Hurley
'Rescued'
Title and signature by E. H. Shackleton
13.5 x 19
Dulwich College

156 p Ocean Camp.

121 L. Hussey
   Letter from Punta Arenas, 3 September 1916
   1 p
   Private collection

Written the day the men arrived, and four days after the rescue, telling 'Mother and Dad' that all are safe. Mentions Blackborow's amputated toes, the Hut on Elephant Island, diet and magnificent reception at Punta Arenas. 'I'm fine & fit & fat. Hope things are alright at home'. Expects to be called up to fight. Shackleton's 'wonderful journey'; survival of banjo: 'Shackleton took to it like a chicken takes to chickweed'.

122 Letter to Percy Blackborow from his brother
   Harold, dated 17.11.15. 2 pp
   Private collection

News from Lime Street, Newport, of the family and of the War. Some neighbours not joining up. Price of bread. The envelope is addressed to *S. Y. Endurance* c/o Magistrate at South Georgia. Shackleton brought mails to the men on Elephant Island. Percy Blackborow was, of course, the stowaway.

123 Shackleton's Polar Medal with ribbon and
   three bars. 10 x 4.5
   Private collection

The Polar Medal was instituted by King Edward VII on the return of *Discovery* in 1904. Frank Wild was the only person to have received four bars, for four expeditions.

124 E. H. Shackleton
   South
   1919
   Dulwich College

125 Worsley
   Endurance
   1931
   Dulwich College. The gift of Emily, Lady Shackleton, 1932

126 Frank Hurley,
   Argonauts of the South
   New York and London, 1925
   Dr Jan Piggott

127 Frank Wild
   Ms. Notes on his Expeditions with
   Shackleton
   7 pp.
   20.5 x 12.5
   Private collection

Wm. Bakewell.

E. Holness

J. V

J. Blackborow.

J. Ives Thom

J. J. Kerr

F. A. Worsley.

McNish

E. H. Shackleton.

Georg. E. Marston.

L. D. A. Hussey.

J. Orde Lees.

R. W. James   Frank W

A. Cheetham

Lieut. W.H Stephenson

T. McCarthy

14 6 NEG

Thomas F McLeod

C J Green

W. How

A. H. Macklin

L Rickinson

No 146

Hubert T. Hudson

L. Greenstreet   J.M Wordie

Frank Hurley

Robert S. Clark

156 ll Digging a cave on Elephant Island for shelter.

128 Ernest Shackleton
Pannikin
Aluminium, 18 x 10
Private collection

See entry for no. 106 above

129 Shackleton
Nansen 'cooker'
Aluminium
78 x 20
Private collection
For the correct terminology and a diagram of 'the Nansen sledging cooker mounted on the Primus', see D. Mawson, *The Home of the Blizzard*, 1915, I, pp. 182–83.

This is the inner compartment, or boiler, referred to by Shackleton, e.g. *South*, p. 205, as the 'cooker'. This is presumably the actual 'small 9-inch aluminium cooker' referred to by Worsley in *Shackleton's Boat Journey* (p. 141). For the inscription inside the lid giving Sørlle's name, see the introduction to this section. Sørlle was the best harpooner in all the Norwegian whaling fleets, and had a vast knowledge of polar ice navigation (A. Lansing, *Endurance*, p. 24).

130 A Scandinavian walnut easy armchair, rectangular back, arm-pads and over-stuffed seat, the back with scroll cresting, orb finials and entablature incised with scrolling foliage, the arms carved

128

130

with lapping coins on baluster supports, on mushroom-topped turned baluster legs with brass castors.
Second half of the 19th. century, 124 x 70 x 66
From the Manager's Office, Stromness.
Dulwich College
Provenance: Salvesen of Leith, Scotland (controllers of Leith Harbour, and owners of the villa, at that time a mess for their staff at Stromness); by whom given to Noel Baker, 1962, by whom presented to Dulwich College.
According to Noel Baker, the sitting-room was about 14 feet square and contained three of these chairs. 'Old hands' at the station confirmed that the chairs had been there since 1916 and earlier (Ms. at Dulwich College).

131 The 'Elephant Island' survivors on arrival at Punta Arenas, September 1916
Photograph. Inscribed by Charles Green, and from his scrapbook
10 x 14
Private collection

132 Shackleton with some of the *Endurance* crew, Buenos Aires, Sept./Oct. 1916
Photograph, 12 x 18
Private collection

133 'Sir Ernest Shackleton's Stirring Appeal for Men for the A.I.F.'
Pamphlet. Issued by the New South Wales Recruiting Committee. Sydney, W. A. Gullick, Govt. Printer.
21 x 29.5

Text of a speech to recruit men to fight in the Australian Imperial Force, made in Sydney, 20 March 1917
Private collection

134 Shackleton
Letter to his son Edward (aged 7), 26 October 1918
Private collection

Dates from Shackleton's assignment on Operation Syren in Russia.

135 Shackleton
Lectures, Philharmonic Hall, Great Portland St., n.d.
Pamphlet, 4 pp., printed in blue.
21 x 26
Private collection

Twice daily: 'the best entertainment in London'; Shackleton personally shows 'marvellous moving pictures' and tells the story of this latest Antarctic expedition; the *Daily Mirror* says, 'as a story it surpasses fiction'.

George Marston (1882–1940)

Marston, artist on the *Nimrod* and the *Endurance*, was also an author (*Antarctic Days*) and a gifted writer of ballads, as has been seen; he was withal an accomplished actor and entertainer, with the speciality of a part *en travesti* – 'in butter muslin and a tow wig' (M. & J. Fisher, *Shackleton*, p. 187) – as is shown in an illustration to *The Heart of the Antarctic.* (I, facing p. 232). Orde-Lees wrote that Marston 'was ever a born actor, & artist, was beautifully made up as an old yokel farm hand in which guise he sang Widdicomb Fair with splendid fine action & later as a human derelict he gave us a bloodcurdling rendering of a gruesome song entitled Johnny Hall' (Diary, p. 176. Dartmouth College Library). He was known by the crew as 'Putty' for his mobile facial features, and by his family as 'Muffin'. From his days as an art student at the Regent Street Polytechnic he knew Shackleton's sisters Helen and Kathleen, and was particularly friendly with the latter. Marston is the subject of a new biography published in March of this year by Stephen Locke (*George Marston: Shackleton's Antarctic Artist*, Hampshire Papers, Hampshire County Council), which has taken advantage of the rich collection of papers and memorabilia deposited at the Hampshire Record Office by his daughter-in-law, Mrs. Veronica Marston, through whose generosity we are able to show in this exhibition the personal drama of a member of the expedition and his family. Kathleen Shackleton writes to him, '*Mind* you do your *own* style of work. Don't mind Ernest. He knows nothing about Art'. We see his anguish and that of his family, when he is separated from sister, mother and father and young wife and baby; we can read the dramatic telegram about his rescue and reassuring letters from Tom Crean and Frank Worsley before the rescue about the party marooned on Elephant Island. Marston's contracts with Shackleton have survived.

Raymond Priestley, a member of the *Nimrod* crew, said that Marston had the 'frame and face of a prize-fighter and the disposition of a fallen angel'. Certainly he was very tough, for all his artistic talent, and was named in the *Endurance* Prospectus as one already chosen to cross the continent. As well as being hardy, he was practical, and the same Prospectus says that he is 'in charge of the clothing and general equipment', which included the sledges and huts. He designed the expedition tent, the 'hoop tent', and tested it in Norway with Shackleton, and mended the men's shoes. Marston, on *Endurance* in the Atlantic, wrote down among his first impressions to his wife, Hazel, that Orde-Lees was 'the most awful snob I ever came across' (Marston papers, Hants. County Record Office, 15A00/A83, 19 August 1914). Orde-Lees, writing down his impressions of the characters on the expedition in his diary, described Marston as 'one of those solid, comfortable, people, square in his nature & appearance, who inspire confidence. His genuineness & integrity are his most outstanding features'. Orde-Lees thought that when Marston did any handicraft the work was beautifully finished, but because of his 'artistic temperament' he did not go out of his way to look for work'; however, 'when it comes his way he does it thoroughly' (7 July 1915, p. 188. Dartmouth College Library). Marston went on in later life to work very hard in the cause of handicrafts and rural industries in Hampshire.

On the *Nimrod* expedition Marston was a member of the party to conquer Mount Erebus, and painted a small oil of the 'Blizzard on Mount Erebus'; he also made many coloured illustrations in watercolour for *The Heart of the Antarctic*, and the watercolour of *Nimrod* for Brocklehurst (no. 84). His work on the

139 *The Blizzard on Mt. Erebus.*

illustration and printing of the *Aurora* has been described earlier. Shackleton describes him in *The Heart of the Antarctic* as 'taking sketches and notes of colours in extreme cold' and being interested in the 'gradations of delicate colours' (I, p. 23). Between the expeditions he taught art, but helped to run Shackleton's office with Frank Wild prior to the departure of the *Endurance*.

Marston's psyche not unnaturally seem to have been profoundly stirred by his experiences on the journey of the boats moving from the ice-floes to Elephant Island and by the desolation of the island; we are able to show, almost as a narrative sequence, images of the boat journeys and the several views of Cape Wild which he made: at Look-out Point, in the view towards the Cape, lay their only hope of being rescued. These images, apart from those in the sketch-book, date from the paintings made shortly after the expedition and some again, most likely, from the Putney studio in the early 1930s. He is seen there in a photograph of that period (reproduced by Locke, op. cit., p. 26) working on a picture of the landing on Elephant Island; another *Endurance* painting hangs on the wall and a large model of *Endurance* is in the foreground. Much of Marston's work (and the model of *Endurance*) was destroyed in a fire at his home. On board *Endurance* Orde-Lees described Marston as working up sketches by artificial light (Diary, op. cit. above, ibid.). Marston lost pictures when *Endurance* went down, but brought back home a number of sketches from Elephant Island. In between appalling conditions, as is obvious from Marston's images, the island had its own splendours, and Shackleton commented in *South* that 'the glow of the dying sun on the mountains filled even the most materialistic of [the men] with wonder and admiration' (p. 232).

Marston's brief text for the catalogue of his Grosvenor Gallery exhibition of May 1922, '*Elephant Island, 1915–16*' tells of the sacrifice of his oils to caulk the life-boats: 'My oil colour was then commandeered to paint the seams of the boats (now our only hope); and in the final escape from the ice, six months later, we doubtless owe some small degree of our safety to those tubes of colour'. He had on Elephant Island, he tells us, a few sheets of paper, half a dozen tubes of watercolour and one pencil. He made the satchel, shown in the exhibition, from 'old tent material, dog harness and a piece of my dog whip'. His sketch-book has also survived, protected as it was by the satchel from damp and decay; in the few days of fair weather Marston used to give his drawings an airing.

136 Self-portrait
Signed and dated 'G. Marston 11.15 am, Sept. 3, 1939'
63 x 53
Hampshire County Museums Service

One of two known self-portraits; this was signed on the day that Britain declared war on Germany.

137 George Edward Marston
Photograph (copy), c. 1914
10 x 7
Scott Polar Research Institute

The fur clothing was used only for this publicity photograph, taken before the expedition sailed.

138 'Marston in his Bed'
The Heart of the Antarctic, I, facing p. 228
Dulwich College

139 The Blizzard on mount Erebus (?). The Antarctic, c. 1908
Oil on plywood packing case, stamped 'BRITISH ANTARCTIC EXPEDITION 1907'
21 x 31.5
Dan and Jonolyn Weinstein, Jamestown, New York

Oil paints froze after about an hour outside; Marston worked fast. The image shows Raymond Priestley's heroic gesture of sleeping outside the three-man tent – there were four men on the sledging expedition to conquer Mount Erebus. He slid down the glacier. Eventually the others helped him into the tent and looked after his frost-bitten feet.

140 S. Y. Endurance Trapped in the Ice in the Weddell Sea
Oil on board
41.9 x 71.2
Provenance: Frank Worsley (d. 1943); sold at Christie's *Exploration and Travel* sale, 17 September 1999, [173]
Dan and Jonolyn Weinstein, Jamestown, New York

Frank Hurley, (*Argonauts of the South*, p. 158): 'The ice-sheet, stretching away a thousand miles to the north, was always changing... The vessel itself was the connecting link between the vast lifeless solitudes of the south, and the living humanity of the north. It was a symbol to all of us, but to me it had a further interest, for, as a factor in any potential composition, it was invaluable'.

141 Camp on the Breaking Pack, Weddell Sea, 1915

(Also known as 'The Reeling Berg. 9 April 1916')
Oil on canvas, 34,3 x 49.5
Provenance: sold at Christie's *Exploration and Travel* Sale, 27 September 1996 [172]
Scott Polar Research Institute. Gift of Miss Barbara Peyton, 1996

See Worsley, *Endurance*, pp. 66–69. Shackleton, *South*, p. 126: ' A big floeberg resting peacefully ahead caught my eye, and half an hour later we had hauled up the boats and pitched camp for the night. It was a fine, big, blue berg with an attractively solid appearance, and from our camp we could get a good view of the surrounding sea and ice. The highest point was about 15 ft. above sea-level. After a hot meal all hands, except the watchman, turned in. Every one was in need of rest after the troubles of the previous night and the unaccustomed strain of the last thirty-six hours at the oars. The berg appeared well able to withstand the battering of the sea, and too deep and massive to be seriously affected by the swell; but it was not as safe as it looked. About midnight the watchman called me and showed me that the heavy north-westerly swell was undermining the ice... Time after time [the next day], so often that a track was formed, Worsley, Wild and I climbed to the highest point of the berg and stared out to the horizon in search of a break in the pack'. Marston's illustration in *South* of this episode ('Hauling up the Boats for the Night', facing p. 121) shows another anxiety, that of bergs on the horizon that might suddenly crash with amazing speed and violence through the ice. The painting appears to show events of April 10 and 11. The episode of the reeling berg is described on p. 128 of *South*: they rushed their boats 'to the edge of the reeling berg and swung them clear of the ice-foot as it rose beneath them'. The *James Caird* was nearly capsized by a blow from below.

142 The *James Caird, Dudley Docker* and
** *Stancomb Wills* in the shelter of the Ice-pack,**
** the Weddell Sea, April 1916.**
  Signed and dated 'G Marston/ 1917', l.r.
  Oil on canvas, 36.3 x 49.5
  Provenance: sold at Christie's *Exploration and*
  Travel sale, 27 September 1996, [173]
  The Earl of Portsmouth

Shackleton, *South*, p. 126: 'The first glimmerings of
dawn came at 6 am'; two hours later the pack opened
and they launched the boats. The *James Caird* was in the
lead, with the *Stancomb Wills* next and the *Dudley Docker*
in the rear. 'Our way was across the open sea, and soon
after noon we swung round the north end of the pack
and laid a course to the westward... Immediately our
boats began to make heavy weather. They shipped
sprays which froze as they fell and covered men and
gear with ice. It was soon clear we could not safely
proceed. I put the *James Caird* round and ran for the
shelter of the pack again, the other boats following'. By
3 p.m. they were back inside the outer line of ice where
the sea was not breaking, but 'all hands were cold and
tired'. See also A. Lansing, *Endurance*, p. 153.

**143 Lookout from a Camp on a Large Ice Floe,
Weddell Sea**
Oil on canvas
53 × 74
Scott Polar Research Institute. Gift of Miss
Barbara Peyton, 1988

144 Navigating a Lead in the Ice Floe of the Weddell Sea

(Also known as 'Sailing towards Elephant Island through the open pack ice')

Signed and dated 'G Marston 1917', l. r.

Oil on canvas

34.3 x 49.5

Provenance: sold at Christie's *Exploration and Travel* sale, 27 September 1996 [175]

Scott Polar Research Institute. Gift of Miss Barbara Peyton, 1996

This is a central image of Shackleton's superhuman endurance. In *South* he underplays his standing at the mast when negotiating leads through the ice, but from Orde-Lees' diary (14 April 1916, p. xiv, Dartmouth College Library) we see the statuesque hero leading his *comitatus*: 'Practically since we had first started Sir Ernest had been standing day and night on the stern-counter of the Caird, only holding on to one of the stays of the little mizen mast conning our course the whole time the boats were under way. How he stood the incessant vigil and exposure is marvellous, but he is a wonderful man, and so is his constitution'. Orde-Lees wrote the following day, 'Sir Ernest had been persuaded to take a little rest, or at least to descend from his exposed position on the stern counter where he had been standing daily for the last five days for 12 hours a day'; Lees also wrote (p. 219) that Shackleton 'did not once lie down for three days'. Marston has not shown the boat as heavily laden with stores as it was in reality.

145 Looking East from Lookout Point with Men and Penguins, Elephant Island, 1916

Oil on canvas

34.3 x 49.5

Scott Polar Research Institute. Gift of Miss Barbara Peyton, 1988

At the top of 'Penguin Hill' at the end of the narrow spit on Elephant Island there was a flag and a look-out for a relief ship: 'The Boss may come today'. From here Shackleton had left to three cheers, after scrutinising the sea for ice (*South*, p. 161).

146 Cape Wild, Elephant Island

Oil on canvas

35.6 x 50.9

Provenance: sold at Christie's *Exploration and Travel* sale, 8 April 1998 [174]

Hampshire County Museums Service

A watercolour of the same view, dated 1916 and inscribed, 'The Coast of Elephant Island (Evening), one of the few bright evenings we experienced during the time we were on Elephant Island' is in the Scott Polar Research Institute. Marston has shown the sea covered in pack ice. This painting shows the 'wonder and admiration' of the Elephant Island view described by Shackleton (see essay above). Cape Wild was named by Shackleton on 16 April 1916. Orde-Lees wrote in his diary: 'We were all up at 4.30 am and by 7 am had launched the boats and commenced loading them for our journey to Cape Wild, the spit which we had found & which Sir Ernest named yesterday' (17 April, p. 377. Dartmouth College Library). For the return six years later to Elephant Island and the attempted return to Cape Wild by members of the party on the *Quest* expedition and for their feelings, see L. Mills, *Frank Wild* p. 305, and Frank Wild, *Shackleton's Last Journey*, pp. 153–168)

146

147 Marston's Elephant Island Sketch-book
13 x 18 (closed)
Mrs. V. Marston. Hampshire County Museums
Service

Showing Cape Wild.

148 Marston's Elephant Island Satchel
Tent canvas and part of a dog harness and whip
33 x 45
Mrs. V. Marston. Hampshire County Museums
Service

See essay above for its use.

149 Marston's Polar Medal, with two bars (*Nimrod*
and *Endurance* expeditions)
10 x 4.5
Mrs. V. Marston. Hampshire County Museums
Service

150 THE MARSTON ARCHIVE (a selection)
All items by courtesy of Mrs. V. Marston.
Lodged with Hampshire County Record Office,
Winchester.

a) **Letter from Helen Shackleton, 4 August 1907.**
15A00/A3

Urges him to accept 'Antarctic job'; 'Ernest feels that
this expedition will reach the South Pole'.

b) **Letter from Shackleton, 13 August 1907.**
15A00/A4

Is ready to appoint artist; asks Marston to call at 9,
Regent Street.

c) **Letter from Marston's Mother, (?)September
1907.** 15A00/A6

Anxieties, and complains about not being consulted
about his joining the expedition.

d) **Letter from his sister Nell, 3 October 1907.**
15A00/A16

147

News of home. Can he spare some money for Mother? Stern face of Shackleton: 'I should be careful not to offend him'; 'I know I won't enjoy a nice fire so much this winter'.

e) Letter from Shackleton, 23 October 1908. 'Strictly Private and Confidential'. 16A00/A47

Should Shackleton not return, Marston to inherit various goods, one of *Nimrod*'s whale boats and any works of art not required for the official account of the expedition.

f) Letter from Kathleen Shackleton, 14 November 1908. 15A00/A48

12, West Hill, Sydenham. News of fellow artists. 'Don't mind Ernest, he knows nothing about Art'.

g) Telegram from Shackleton to Mrs. Marston, 30 December 1913. 15A00/A79

Thanks her for letting her husband go. 'You can rest assured that we will all come back safe no precaution will be neglected and all will be well. I need him badly'.

h) Agreement between Shackleton and Marston, 9 August 1914. 15A00/B35

Includes terms for any pictures or paintings made on the *Endurance* expedition.

i) Letter from Marston to his daughter Heather for her second birthday (written at Buenos Aires in advance), 23 October 1915. 15A00/A90

Sketch of a seal and a pup to illustrate a (fictitious) story.

j) Letter to Hazel Marston from Tom Crean, R.M.S. *Orita*, 3 July 1916. 15A00/A92

Assures her that George is well, and positive that they will rescue them from Elephant Island. George 'looking fit and well' when he last saw him.

k) Letter from Frank Worsley to Hazel Marston, R.M.S. *Orita*, Punta Arenas, 4 July 1916. 15A00/A93

Arranging the third attempt to rescue the men, who ten weeks ago had six weeks of food left and any seal and penguin that they might catch. George withstood the 150 mile journey to Elephant Island well. The men must be worried that the *Caird* party did not make it.

l) Telegram from Ernest Perris to Hazel Marston, 4 September 1916. 15A00/A95

All are saved and well.

m) Ballad, 'They sailed there in a ship Sir'. 15A00/B10

Describes *Endurance* sinking and the days when marooned on Elephant Island. Transcribed in the section of catalogue about *Endurance*, above, pp. 96–97.

n) Photograph of a painting showing the Landing on Elephant Island. 15A00/B19 Signed and dated 1935. Illus. p. 94

The painting is shown on the easel in a photograph of Marston's Putney studio in the same collection, c. 1930s.

156 k Frank Hurley aloft, Ernest Shackleton on deck of *Endurance* (detail).

Frank Hurley (1885–1962)

Hurley is the poet of Antarctic velvet black and dazzling white, the laureate photographer of *Endurance*. The ship appears at first as the elegant 'bride of the sea', in Hurley's own phrase from *Argonauts of the South* (p. 124); then beset, as the doomed symbol of humanity and its enterprise pitted against vast and white windswept null death-landscapes; finally in the death-throes of wrecked hope. Hurley's studies of the fortitude and cheer of the men, and a few images of misery defied on Elephant Island, taken with the box camera, confirm the written evidence of superhuman endurance.

The revival of interest in Shackleton has been closely involved with the now almost universal recognition of the genius of his photographer and 'kinematographer'. This has been brought about by the exhibitions at the American Museum of Natural History in Washington and at the National Geographic Society in New York in 1998–99, and now elsewhere in the United States, by the publication of Caroline Alexander's *The Endurance* in 1998, and by the British Film Institute's work in restoring the print of *South* in the same year. Hurley was a metaphorical and several times almost a real martyr to his art, clinging to the bowsprit, climbing a yard arm; making a platform under the jib boom to film the ship breaking through the ice, with the unforgettable image of the cruciform shadow of the prow (Shackleton, *South*, p. 9); developing glass negatives and film in near impossible conditions, and braving deathly cold waters and mushy ice, bare from head to waist, to reclaim (with Walter How's help) the canisters of film from the sinking ship which were still in the refrigerator in the hold. As is well known, Shackleton and Hurley together went through 600 glass negatives on the ice and smashed all but 150 of what they thought were the best, so as to have no second thoughts that would risk weighing down the boats.

Hurley was young, celebrating his 29th birthday on *Endurance* in October 1914, and was a source of amused surprise to his companions. Worsley wrote that he was 'a marvel – with cheerful Australian profanity he perambulates alone aloft & everywhere, in the most dangerous and slippery places he can find, content & happy at all times but cursing if he can get a good or novel picture. Stands bare & hair waving in the wind, where we are gloved & helmeted, he snaps his snap or winds his handle turning out curses of delight & pictures of Life by the fathom' (R. Huntford, *Shackleton*, p. 400). His monthly 'lantern chats' on *Endurance* were popular, especially 'Peeps in Java' with waving palms and native ladies (A. Lansing, *Endurance*, p. 43).

Lennard Bickel's *In Search of Frank Hurley* (Melbourne, 1980) has recovered the story of the boy who ran away from school and home at the age of thirteen, and recounted his many travels and adventures. A fuller study of his interest in 'composite photographs' and his genius as a war photographer – 'Menin Road' from the First World War is surely one of the greatest photographs ever taken – should follow. Hurley's own diaries and his two books not surprisingly show great sensitivity and thoughtfulness about images, for example where he talks about the subjects of his photographs:

> I conceived the ambition of making some pictures of the *Endurance* that would *endure*, and I spent days and weeks studying her from all angles and positions. She was never twice the same. She was indeed a lady of infinite variety. Some times she looked stark and grim, with bare poles and black ropes, then overnight, snow would fall and the gaunt mast and their cordage would be powdered with dazzling white. Again, when a pool formed amongst the ice-floes, volumes of dense frost vapours condensed on the rigging; line and spar, stowed sails, braces, anchor chains, glittered with countless tiny ice-crystals which flashed like diamonds. But perhaps never did the ship look so beautiful as when the bright moonlight etched her in inky silhouette, or transformed her into a vessel from fairyland. During the winter months, when we lost the sun for ninety days and everything was encased in ice, I took a series of flashlight pictures with the temperature at seventy degrees below freezing point (*Argonauts of the South*, pp. 158–59).

On Elephant Island the images taken with the pocket camera and the last three spools of film, of which more are shown in this exhibition than have been published, are moving. To see the faces and figures of Shackleton's men that one has read about come to life in the film *South* is an extraordinary experience.

Hurley's diaries are published. Along with his two books on the expedition, *Argonauts of the South* (1925) and its second version, *Shackleton's Argonauts* (1948),

they confirm Hurley as a marvellous writer. Hurley's account of the boat journey from the ice to Elephant Island is wonderful; this is how he describes the arrival on Elephant Island:

> We were a pitiful sight; the greater number terribly frost-bitten and half delirious. Some staggered aimlessly about and flung themselves down on the beach, hugging the very rocks and trickling the pebbles through their hands as though they were nuggets of gold. It is hard to describe the joy we felt, walking on land, feeling and looking upon solid rocks after having lived through the terrible experiences of the past sixteen months. To feel land under our feet – land that would not split and disintegrate!
>
> And then to fall asleep; to rest unperturbed; to turn over and hearken to the music of the surf; the swirl of the ice-blocks; the croak of the penguins; to dream with hope of the future; to experience the unspeakable joy of awakening in the morning to find we were still on something solid, something that had not drifted miles in the night. It was the realisation of all our hopes. It was Heaven. Nothing else mattered. A terrible chapter in our lives had ended; we scarcely cared what was to open the next. (p. 245)

Five albums are reputed to have been made. Hurley took one in a taxi to Buckingham Palace. It is not known when and from whom this album came to the College.

152 Frank Hurley
Photographs of Scenes and Incidents in connection with the Happenings to the Weddell Sea Party. 1914. 1915. 1916.
79 photographs, lithographed list of contents, title-page and list of the 17 'Staff'. Half-bound in black leather with grey cloth sides.
31 X 41 X 7.5
Dulwich College

Given by Miss Hale, a member of the Shackleton circle and a friend of Ernest Perris, to her nephew Norman Pennant in 1923; presented to Dulwich College by Mr. Pennant (of Natal, South Africa), 1973.

151 Frank Hurley
The Imperial Trans-Antarctic Expedition. Commander: Sir Ernest Shackleton, C.V.O., Photographs of Scenes and Incidents in connection with the Happenings to the Weddell Sea Party. 1914. 1915. 1916.
78 photographs and a hand-lettered title-page, listing the 17 'Staff', i.e. officers. Bound in black crushed morocco, tooled on the cover 'The Shackleton Expedition'; all edges gilt.
31 X 41 X 7
Dulwich College

153 *Endurance*
Gaumont-British Picture Corporation Ltd.: illustrated pamphlet to accompany the film
n.d. (1933)
31 X 23
Private collection

The film of *South* was first issued in 1919, with a spoken commentary by Shackleton, at the Philharmonic Hall in London and on tour; this brochure is for the composite film produced in 1933 by W. and F. Film Service (after Gaumont-British) of *Endurance* material and some material from the *Quest*. In 1955 all materials were acquired by the British Film Institute. (See M. & J. Fisher, *Shackleton*, p. 440 (n.).

154 Frank Hurley
Argonauts of the South
New York and London, 1925
Dr. Jan Piggott

155 THE HURLEY COLLECTION

Dulwich College would like to thank Atlas Limited Editions for the kind loan to the exhibition of twenty framed photographs by Hurley. These prints are from *The Hurley Collection*, a limited edition series of thirty-five images printed using the original negatives in the possession of the Royal Geographical Society, these being the original negatives which Hurley salvaged from the wreck of *Endurance* as it was being crushed. All prints are strictly limited to 400 copies. In addition, a special signed edition of the twenty images is also available exclusively through Atlas Limited Editions. All prints in this exhibition series are available as a set or as single prints specially signed by the Hon. Alexandra Shackleton.

For more information about *The Hurley Collection* or to order prints from the Collection contact:

> Atlas Gallery,
> 55–57 Tabernacle Street,
> London EC2A 4AA.
> Tel: (44) 020 7490 4540
> Fax: (44) 020 7490 4514
> e-mail: order@atlasgallery.com
> web: www.atlasgallery.com

A note on titles: where original ones exist, i.e. in albums, what is presumed to be Hurley's own title is given, between inverted commas. As this might make for confusion in identifying the Atlas prints, the number of the Atlas print from their catalogue, *The Hurley Collection*, will be found in square brackets.

a) Portrait of Frank Hurley. [1]
b) 'The Cinematographer (Hurley) at Work'. [2]
c) 'A Lake among Leads in the Pack Ice'. [3]
d) 'Evening in the Pack Ice, 9 December 1914'. [4]
e) ' "Endurance" Fast in the Sea of Ice'. [9]
f) 'New Leads Covered with Ice Flowers in Early Spring'. [11]
g) In the Ice. [12]
h) 'Ice Conditions in August 1915'. [13]
i) The *Endurance* under Full Sail. [15]
j) Wild and Chums. [18]

k) Midwinter Dinner, 22 June 1915. [20]
l) 'Round the Nightwatchman's Fire'. [21]
m) ' "Endurance" at Midwinter, 1915 (taken by flashlight)'. [24]
n) 'Sir Ernest Shackleton examining the Effects of the Pressure about a Week before the Ship was finally Crushed'. [26]
o) ' "Endurance" Crushed by the Ice and Sinking into the Waters Below'. [27]
p) 'Sir Ernest Shackleton and Frank Hurley in Front of the Tent at Patience Camp on the Ice Floe'. [28]
q) 'Frank Wild Examining the Wreckage of the "Endurance".' [29]
r) Relaying the *James Caird* [30]
s) South Georgia 2. [32]
t) South Georgia Mountains [33]

156 Frank Hurley
Royal Geographical Society Prints
On loan to the Exhibition from the collection of the Royal Geographical Society Picture Library, who have held the original glass plate negatives from this expedition since 1929.

ENDURANCE

a) The crew of the *Endurance* taken on the bow
b) On the bow of the *Endurance*, 9 December 1914
c) Sir Ernest Shackleton's cabin on *Endurance*
d) A morning in the Ritz, on board the *Endurance* in Midwinter
e) Dr. Hussey and Frank Hurley playing chess on board the *Endurance*
f) On the deck of the *Endurance*
g) The Rockery. The Scientific Laboratory with Dr. Hussey and Reginald James
h) Skiing on the ice, 14 January 1915
i) On the ice
j) Alfred Cheetham and Tom Crean
k) Frank Hurley aloft, Ernest Shackleton on deck of *Endurance*
l) On an ice-floe, trying to cut *Endurance* free, February 1915
m) The crew cutting ice
n) Look-out post with Union Flag
o) Ocean Camp [distant]
p) Ocean Camp [close]
q) 'Loneliness'. Ocean Camp in the distance, October 1915

A HURLEY GALLERY

156 b On the bow of *Endurance*, 9 December 1914.

156 c Sir Ernest Shackleton's cabin on *Endurance*.

Leonard Hussey and his Dog Team, September 1915 (Royal Geographical Society).

156 h Skiing on the ice, 14 January 1915.

156 m The crew cutting the ice.

Frank Wild beside *Endurance* during her final break-up (Royal Geographical Society).

156 x First landing on Elephant Island.

156 z The first meal on Elephant Island and the first hot meal for several days.

156 ee Launching the *James Caird*.

156 bb Loading the *James Caird* with shingles and boulders for ballast, 23 April 1916.

156 nn Whaling Station, South Georgia

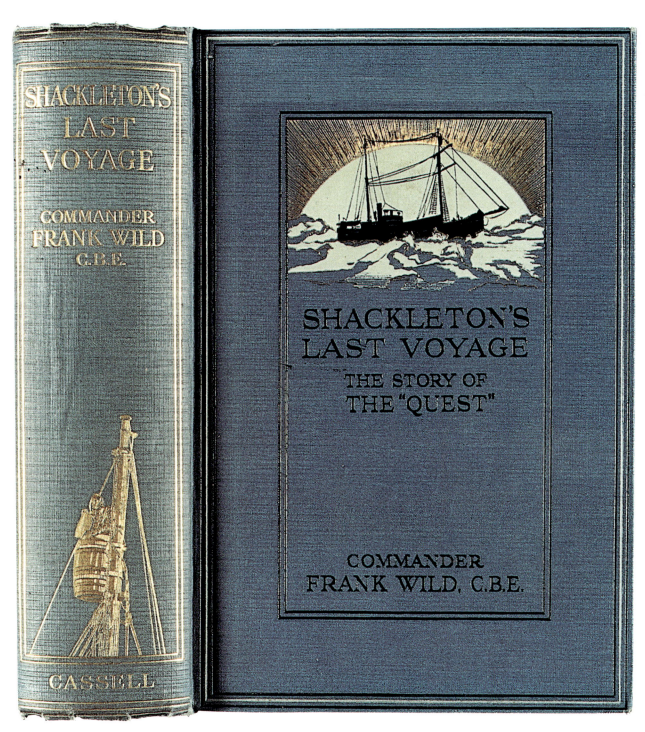

174 'The Last Farewell.'

Quest and Death

The Shackleton–Rowett Expedition (1921–22)

We are the fools who could not rest
In the dull earth we left behind,
But burned with passion for the South
And drank strange frenzy from its wind,
The world where wise men live at ease
Fades from our regretful eyes,
And blind across uncharted seas
We stagger on our enterprise.

St. John Lucas, 'The Ship of Fools',
as quoted by E. H. S.

Shackleton's last journey of exploration was made in a wooden Norwegian sealer and whaler, renamed the *Quest*. At first he had planned to go north in her, on an expedition to the Beaufort Sea in the Arctic, which was to be financed by the Canadian government. However, this plan fell through, and he found a new backer in an old Dulwich friend, John Quiller Rowett (1876–1924), who had amassed a considerable fortune by what amounted to a monopoly to supply rum to the Royal Navy, and had given generously to philanthropic causes: agricultural research, medicine, dentistry and chemistry. The Shackleton-Rowett Expedition aimed to reach and map out new land in the Enderby Quadrant in Antarctica. Shackleton's old friend and later his biographer, H. R. Mill, was unenthusiastic; he wrote in his *Autobiography*:

> Each time I met Shackleton I found him less accurate in judging how to fit his great ambitions to the moderate possibility of the little vessel, the *Quest*, which he had obtained for the Arctic venture, and was now going to employ in the very different seas of the South. He was cramming her with new devices and elaborate gear that I felt could not be worked effectively in the confined space of the tiny craft; and I was greatly depressed when I inspected the miserable little *Quest* at Hay's Wharf by London Bridge (p.153).

Sectional pictures of the ship from magazines show a trim, if cramped outfit. The ship sailed with Kipling's poem 'If' on a brass plate placed in front of the bridge, affirming (as if in an extended slogan) its strictures about manhood. The actual pieces, the relics, of the *Quest* assembled here – the clock, crow's nest and brass plaque – seem to convey their own symbolism of elements in Shackleton's life, signifying the passing of time, the explorer's lookout among the ice and the importance to Shackleton of poetry.

The expedition had originally modest intentions; there was apparently some hope of Shackleton's that they would find minerals. There were bad omens, such as a serious leak in the boiler between Rio and South Georgia, and the expedition was of course cut short by Shackleton's heart attacks and his death in his cabin off South Georgia. The men in severe snowing conditions made a memorial cairn surmounted by a cross on the headland overlooking Grytviken harbour with cere-monial actions resembling the burial of an Anglo-Saxon chief; this was preserved on cinema film (*Southward on the Quest*, 1922, British Film Institute); 'no one grudged the labour and time spent, for it was the last job we should do for the Boss' (Wild, p. 193). The magnificent funeral in Montevideo, and the interment at Grytviken were to follow. The expedition is remembered thus exactly as it figures in the title of Frank Wild's commemorative account of the expedi-tion (following what was by now the standard practice of the leader of the expedition publishing a book): it was *Shackleton's Last Voyage*. Shackleton 'went about his preparations with the heart of a boy, though old friends saw in his face signs of the wear and tear of his long years of unceasing hardship and toil' (H. R. Mill, *Life of Sir Ernest Shackleton*, p. 272).

The *Quest* took advantage of advances in technology, and was moreover equipped with an Avro 'Baby' sea-plane; the crow's nest and overalls for the watch were even fitted with electric heating (M. &. J. Fisher, *Shackle-ton*, p. 449; H .R. Mill, *Life of Sir Ernest Shackleton*, p. 272). The 'gadgets' led to some mockery. There is Pathé Gazette and Gaumont newsreel footage of the *Quest* leaving St. Katharine's Dock and going under Tower Bridge at the thronged farewell and godspeed from the Londoners (British Film Institute), as is shown in Charles Dixon's painting where you can almost hear the excited crowds. The film *Southward on the Quest* has a scene of Shackleton on board the ship washing his Alsatian wolf-hound puppy 'Query' in a bucket.

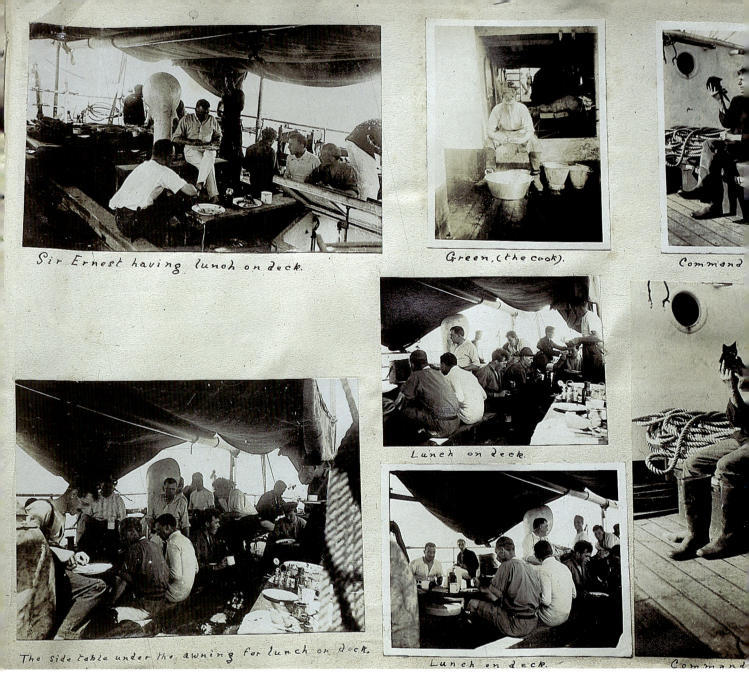

Sir Ernest having lunch on deck.

Green, (the cook).

Command

Lunch on deck.

The side table under the awning for lunch on deck.

Lunch on deck.

Command

179 Scenes on the deck of the *Quest*.

The crowds on St. Katharine's Wharf waving good-bye.

179 The crowds on St. Katharine's Wharf waving good-bye.

Even Mill had to agree that Shackleton had assembled a 'splendid body of helpers', including eight comrades from the *Endurance*: Green, Hussey, Kerr, McIlroy, McLeod, Macklin, Wild and Worsley. (Two members of the *Endurance* crew had been killed in the War; the remarkable Orde-Lees incidentally, as a direct consequence of his experiences on the ice and on Elephant Island, had become a Roman Catholic). The camaraderie of the expedition, of the Boss with the Boys, is well illustrated by the informal photographs in the *Quest* album of lunch on deck. Wild wrote that, 'Sir Ernest seemed to be enjoying the quiet, the freedom and the mental peace of our small self-contained world. I think he liked to find himself surrounded by his own men, and he was always at his best when he had a definite objective to go for' (p. 27). In the still nights off Rio de Janeiro 'we gathered outside the surgeon's cabin whilst Hussey strummed tunes on his banjo. The Boss loved these little musical gatherings' (p. 43).

The night before Shackleton died, 4 January 1922, after a 'cheery' evening, according to Wild's account, the Boss said on retiring to his cabin that the next day they should keep Christmas; this was because December 25 had been passed in a furious gale, 'the most frightful storm in all Shackleton's experience' (Mill, op. cit., p. 277), and they had eaten only bully-beef sandwiches. The diary entries for the four final evenings of Shackleton's life make very moving reading: in spite of his 'deeply probing' anxieties and many things going awry, he noted that the spirit of all on board was 'sound and good', and quoted again favourite lines from Browning:

> *There are two points in the adventures of a diver,*
> *One when a beggar he prepares to plunge,*
> *One when a prince he rises with his pearl.*

'Ah me! the years that have gone since in the pride of young manhood I first went forth to the fight. I grow old and tired, but must always lead on'. The image which he wrote down a few hours before his death seems quite supernatural in its aptness:

> *In the darkening twilight I saw a lone star hover*
> *Gem-like above the bay.*

The crew of the *Quest* when they continued on their journey experienced a brief and almost a commemorative besetting in the ice (off 'Ross's Appearance of Land'), and, ostensibly to find sea-elephants in sufficient numbers to supply them with blubber as fuel, Wild took the ship to Elephant Island where they had landed eight years before, recalling at that point in his book the 'indomitable will' of Shackleton 'who had overcome every obstacle and surmounted each difficulty as it arose', and where he 'lay down on the shingle and had his first sleep for eight days' (p. 155). Approaching Cape Wild they saw, as in Marston's paintings shown in the exhibition, the 'rosy glare' and the 'reddish-golden glow' on the snow and ice of the Cape.

This section of the exhibition shows glimpses of Shackleton's social life after returning from the *Endurance* expedition, at a garden party in Sydenham or at Ely Place staying with John Quiller Rowett, or magnificently seated in a leather armchair below a suitably imperial swag and a tassel. The later fortunes of the *James Caird*, which he gave or sold to Rowett are shown in pictures of the boat at Ely Place, at the Middlesex hospital, and on the roof garden of Selfridges. A drawing of his parents signed by his son Edward and his daughter Cecily shows a rather shadowy paternal figure, dressed in morning suit and top hat.

In the small Lutheran church at Grytviken there were two bronze wreaths placed there by Hussey: one 'a token of fraternal affection from Old Alleynians in the River Plate'; the other, from King George V and the British people. The former, described as a 'bronze plaque', along with 'bronze wreaths' filled a carriage at the funeral service (*Alleynian*, L, 1, no. 368, February 1933, p.72). There was also a flower wreath placed there by Mrs. Aarberg, the doctor's wife and the only woman resident on South Georgia (Wild, *Shackleton's Last Voyage* p. 194). There followed the Memorial Service in St. Paul's, and in May 1923 the Shackleton Memorial Fund was opened by John Quiller Rowett who proposed to raise funds for permanent memorials to Shackleton in London and in other towns where he was particularly associated, to provide for the education of his children and to encourage exploration. The capital raised helped to educate his children and to support Shackleton's mother. When his mother died in 1929, a permanent memorial was proposed, to be paid for from the capital in the Fund. Eventually, in January 1932 C. S. Jagger's statue of Shackleton, surely among the greatest of twentieth-century sculptures, was placed in a niche at the Royal Geographical Society. It was originally intended to be mounted on a plinth that was to have been designed by Jagger's associate Lutyens, and to have been placed in a London square seen from all sides – the empty plinth now in Trafalgar Square comes to mind. [M. & J. Fisher, *Shackleton*, p. 486 are wrong in

saying that Lutyens designed the statue]. The photo-graph of the statue in the sculptor's studio, though theatrically lit, contrasts with the more null impression given today by its frontal view in a niche, set too high at the Kensington Gore end of Exhibition Road.

157 Charles Dixon (1872–1934)
      R. Y. S. Quest **Leaving St. Katharine's Dock,**
      September 18, 1921
      Watercolour
      Signed and dated 1921
      85 x 138
      By courtesy of Maggs Bros., Ltd.

Charles Dixon, a well-known marine artist, was the son of the artist Alfred Dixon. He first exhibited at the Royal Academy at the age of sixteen. A yachtsman, living at Itchenor, where he was a Founder Member of the Yacht Club, he contributed pictures of many such scenes to the *Graphic* and *Illustrated London News* &c.

The Times for 19 September 1921, p. 10, describes the send-off as 'a perfect din', with the 'sirens of steamers' and ' the ringing cheers of thousands of Londoners': 'a triumphal progress'. She left the Dock at 1 o'clock, towed by the tug *Adder*, and passed under the Tower Bridge. Worsley (*Endurance*, 1931, p. 268) commented, 'As we steamed down the river the vessels lined along the banks and coming upstream dipped their ensigns and blew their whistles to us. It was a great send-off, and Shackleton, who took a boyish delight in being made a fuss of, was delighted'. Shackleton had been elected a member of the Royal Yacht Squadron, and flew the White Ensign.

158 The Crow's Nest of *Quest*
      Wood, with metal fixings, rope and a com-
      memorative brass plaque
      Barrel, 120 x 75 diam.
      By kind permission of the Vicar and Parochial Church Council of All Hallows by the Tower, London EC3.

The crow's nest plays a particularly important part in Antarctic exploration, as the Captain needs to manoeu-vre among floes in the pack-ice (see Huntford, *Shackleton*, p. 53). The crow's nest is pictured in a splendid photograph by Macklin of 'Commander Wild at the Masthead', facing p. 108 of Frank Wild, *Shackleton's Last Voyage*; the book also has the crow's nest (with what appear to be Shackleton's features on the man standing in it) in the fine design blocked on the broad spine of the book (p. 141).

The crow's nest was presented to All Hallows Church by the Rev. Philip Thomas Byard ('Tubby')

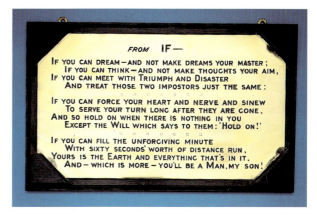

160 Plaque, inscribed with quotation (three verses) from Kipling's poem 'If'
Bronze on wood
30 x 80
Private collection

Clayton, C.H., M.C., the famous chaplain who established Talbot House for the Allied soldiers at the Ypres salient, and Founder of the subsequent Toc H movement. Clayton was Vicar at All Hallows from 1923–63. There appears to be no evidence as to how he acquired it. It is possible that the Vicar of All Hallows took part in a ceremonial blessing or send-off, as exploration ships traditionally carried down the Thames the flag of the Bishop in whose diocese the dock lay. St. Katharine's Dock is right by the church, which is plainly visible in Charles Dixon's painting. The crow's nest originally had a contraption for electric heating (see essay above).

Shackleton first met Kipling at the time of the publication of *O. H. M. S.* in 1900 (H. R. Mill, *The Life of Sir Ernest Shackleton*, p. 54); latterly he had stayed at Bateman's with Emily. The code expressed in the poem finds echoes in Shackleton's diaries, e.g., 'We had to play the game to the utmost and Providence will look after us' (*Nimrod* diary, 8 January 1909, quoted Huntford, *Shackleton*, p. 271). Shackleton had the poem framed on the wall of his cabin on *Endurance*, (see, to l., in Hurley's photo of the cabin, R.G.S. Neg. C61). Leonard Hussey's parody of the poem, listing the ordeals of keeping your head on the *Quest* expedition, is printed by Wild, op. cit., p. 34).

161 Rudyard Kipling
'If—'
Macmillan and Co., 1914, 4 pp.
Private collection

159 The clock from Sir Ernest Shackleton's Cabin on the *Quest*
Inscribed 'To the Boss from the Boys'
20 x 20 x 10
Private collection

The Times, 17 September, 1921, 'The *Quest* sails today': 'In Sir Ernest's tiny cabin on the deck is a handsome clock bearing the inscription, "From the boys to the boss", while under the bridge deck is a brass plate bearing three verses from Kipling's "If" '.

Sir E. Shackleton giving the order to cast off.

Shackleton kept copies of this very same pamphlet printing of the poem to give to people whom he talked to about poetry.

162 'Southward Ho! A Little Ship Bound on a 30,000 Mile Voyage to Antarctic Seas'
The Illustrated London News, **17 Sept. 1921**
(Photographic copy)
'Drawn by our Special Artist, W. B. Robinson, after a Visit to the "Quest"'
Dulwich College

163 Charles Green's Enamel Cup from *Quest*
With device 'R. Y. S. Quest'
5.1 x 10.2
Private collection

164 The *James Caird* at Ely Place, c. 1922
Photograph in Album, 24 x 30
Private collection

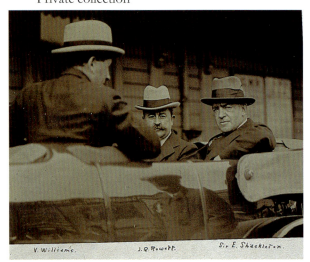

V. Williams.   J. Q. Rowett.   Sir E. Shackleton.

179 John Quiller Rowett and Sir Ernest Shackleton.

The children of John Quiller Rowett (Helen, Caroline and John Penrose) playing inside the boat.

165 The *James Caird* at the Middlesex Hospital
Photograph
Private collection

166 The *James Caird* at the roof garden of Selfridges
Photograph (copy)
Mr. Roderick Dunnett

167 Ernest Shackleton
Letter to 'Ellie', Mrs. John Quiller Rowett
Marlborough Club, 18 July, 1921
4 PP
Private collection

' "Never the lowered banner,
Never the lost Endeavour". I like these lines, Ernest'.

168 [(Sir) George Hubert Wilkins, photographer?] Kinemette (distributor)
Shackleton's Last Expedition. Southward in the 'Quest'
Boxed set of slides and viewer, London 1922.
52 slides.
Box 7.4 x 7.4 x 16.8
Private collection

169 New Testament belonging to Charles Green
48mo., Scripture Gift Mission and Naval and Military Bible Society
n.d., inscribed 'Quest R. Y. S. 1921–22', with signature of C. J. Green
Dulwich College, the gift of J. Markham, 1997

170 Charles Green and Ernest Shackleton aboard the *Quest* in London, September 1921
Photograph
Private collection

171 The Fiftieth Anniversary of the Sailing of the *Endurance*, London 19 June, 1964
Photograph, by Mrs. Elizabeth Rajala
Charles Green, William Bakewell, Dr. A Macklin, Lionel Greenstreet, Dr. J. McIlroy, Walter How (with back to camera)
Private collection

172 Shackleton's *Quest* Diary
Bound in red morocco, with brass clasp
Private collection

Opened at the last entry, written the night he died, 4 January 1922. The short diary is transcribed in extracts in F. Wild, *Shackleton's Last Voyage*, pp. 18–23 and 58–59.

173 E. H. Shackleton
Poem 'To "General" Gerald Lysaght A.B.,
El Rey de Portugal'
25 x 20.5, on mount. India ink on photographic paper (from the dark room of *Quest*?) with images of Shackleton on the bridge of *Quest*, inscribed 'The Unceasing Watch', and also showing the Kent 'Clear View Screen', which 'by centrifugal force throws off all hail, sleet, rain &c.' (see illustration from *Illustrated London News*, no. 162 above) and a lifebuoy. The poem is printed on p. 35–36 of Wild's *Shackleton's Last Voyage*, which refers to this original 'illuminated card' presented to Lysaght, with its mount showing the White Ensign and R. Y. S. burgee. Dated 26.10.21, at St. Vincent, and signed by Shackleton and sixteen members of the expedition.

Gerald Stuart Lysaght (1869–1951) met Shackleton in 1899, when he was a passenger on the *Tantallon Castle* on which Shackleton was the Fourth Officer. He was a wealthy steelmaker from Scunthorpe who helped to finance the *Nimrod* expedition, and was later High Sheriff of Somerset. He joined the ship as far as St. Vincent, and was given Shackleton's cabin. Wild mentions him as a 'keen yachtsman' (p. 17), saying that 'he was very popular with all of us, for in addition to his support of expedition affairs he had taken a personal interest in every member of the expedition'. Shackleton noted in his diary that Lysaght spent long hours at the wheel (Wild, op. cit., p. 21). Shackleton, Lysaght and two others were the only ones to escape serious sea-sickness on board (H. R. Mill, *The Life of Sir Ernest Shackleton*, p. 274. The poem talks of the companionship of Lysaght with the 'little band' of the *Quest* among gales, the ship's 'reeling spars' sweeping past the steady stars in the 'storm-wracked night', and passing great liners without envy,

> *For you are one with the sea in its joy and misery.*
> *You follow its lure.*

174 Southward on the Quest. Shackleton's Last
Antarctic Expedition

'Scala Souvenir' Booklet
29 x 36. 8 pp.
Dulwich College

175 Frank Wild
Shackleton's Last Voyage. The Story of the
'Quest' ('From the official journal and private diary kept by Dr. A. H. Macklin')
Cassell, 1923
Dr. Jan Piggott

176 Balaclava
taken by Dr. A. H. Macklin (later O.B.E., M.C., M.D., R.A.M.C.) on the *Quest* expedition
Woollen, Cash's name-tape with initials 'A.M.'.
39 x 32
Presented by Mrs. Helen Carpenter, 1997
Dulwich College

177 Ernest Shackleton
Telegram to John Quiller Rowett, 10 October
1922
Lisbon
Private collection

Quest ready for sea, but waiting for wind change or drop... useless burning coal against a head sea.

189

178 Leonard Hussey
Letter to his parents, 2 February 1922
Headed writing-paper from Hotel La Alhambra,
Montevideo. 1p.
Private collection

Bringing home Shackleton's dead body; being treated
like a king here. Has had scores of people dying on his
hands in the past, 'but this was different'. 'I tried to
inject some ether to stimulate his heart, but in 3 minutes he was dead'. A 'first-class passage to England in
the biggest R. M. S. steamer afloat'.

179 *Quest* photograph Album, (i)
33 X 44.5
Private collection

180 John Quiller Rowett Family Album, (ii)
24 X 30
Private Collection

181 John Quiller Rowett
Newspaper photograph
Set by McC. Christison in his grangerised volume
of *The Alleynian* for 1921–22
Dulwich College

182 Shackleton at the Binnacle of *Quest*, 1921
Photograph, signed 'E. H. Shackleton'
16 X 11.5
Private collection

183 On board [?]*Quest*, Rio de Janiero,
November/December, 1921: McIlroy,
Shackleton and Wild
Photograph, signed by McIlroy, Shackleton and
Wild, showing visitors
15.5 X 19.5
Private collection

184 On board *Quest*: McIlroy, Carr, Wild and
Macklin
Photograph, signed by the men
10.5 X 13.5
Private collection

Probably taken when the ship became beset.

185 Frank Wild
Lecture pamphlet
'The Story of the "Quest" will be told by Comdr.
Frank Wild, C.B.E., Queen's Hall, November 27
and 30, 1922, with lantern slides and Kinemato-
graphic film'. With six photographs, two relating

194

to the Shackleton Memorial at Grytviken harbour.
4 pp.
Private collection

186 Press Cutting book, *Quest* Expedition, (i)
25.5 x 31.8
Private collection

187 Press cutting book, *Quest* expedition, (ii)
25.5 x 31.8
Private collection

188 Ernest Shackleton
Studio Portrait Photograph, Speaight, 1914
28.5 x 20
Dulwich College

189 Ernest Shackleton with his sisters
Photograph
Date unknown
Private collection

190 Ernest Shackleton
Studio Portrait Photograph
Claude Harris, 1920, 20 x 15
Dulwich College, the gift of the Hon. Alexandra
Shackleton

191 Reginald Granville Eves, R.A. (1876–1941)
Ernest Henry Shackleton, 1921
Oil on canvas
59.5 x 48.5
National Maritime Museum

Eves painted portraits and topographical subjects. He
studied at the Slade, lived in Yorkshire and from 1900
worked in London. He was encouraged by John Singer
Sargent. He painted celebrities such as Thomas Hardy
and Max Beerbohm. Elected R.A. 1939.

Eves, at Dame Jane Stancomb-Wills's instigation,
did three portraits of Shackleton. One of these was
commissioned and paid for by her, with the hope that
the National Portrait Gallery would accept it. Although
one of the three pictures is indeed now in the National
Portrait Gallery, this is the painting which belonged to
Janet Stancomb-Wills.

192 Ernest Shackleton
Portrait photograph, c. 1920
Private collection

Seated in leather armchair, with a swag above

191

193 Ernest Shackleton
Portrait photograph, c. 1920
Private collection

Seated in leather armchair, with tassel above

**194 Ernest Shackleton at a Garden Party,
'St. Michael's Sale, 22 July 1914'
'Mrs. Denton's Garden'**
Photograph on post card, stamped 'Watson.
Sydenham'. 8.5 x 13
Private collection

Taken shortly before the departure of *Endurance*.
Shackleton behaved with boyish enthusiasm at such
events, for example at a later Eastbourne camp of Girl
Guides with Emily: 'a large lunch basket accompanied
the party, and when it was opened the *pièce de resistance*
was found to be a big toy penguin, which the explorer
had carefully packed, with a carving-knife and fork'
(Mill, *Life of Sir Ernest Shackleton*, p. 269).

195 Coconut, silver-mounted as sugar-bowl
Coconut won at garden-party to raise money for
the *Quest* expedition, by Ernest Shackleton, and
given to Frank Wild's niece, 1920. Silver
mountings made by J. Grose, of Garrard's, the
girl's father. 16,5 x 11.5
Private collection

**196 Edward Arthur Alexander, later Rt. Hon.
Lord Shackleton, K.G., A.C., O.B.E., F.R.S.**
(1911–94) and **Cecily Shackleton** (1906–57)
Drawing of their parents
Juvenile drawing signed 'C. Shackleton + Eddie'
National Maritime Museum

This drawing and the cards (Nos. 26, 67 & 68) were
given to Miss Margery Grace Smith by the Shackleton
family after she tended the children for a year.

193

197 'An Explorer's Home. Chat with Lady Shackleton', *Mother's Weekly*, n.d. (1916/17)
Dulwich College

On the bringing up of her children and their characteristics; reunion with Ernest at docks after *Discovery*.

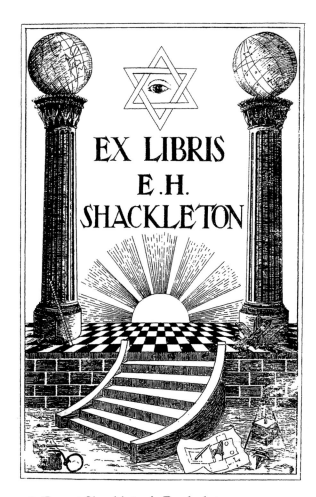

198 **Ernest Shackleton's Bookplate**
In a copy of Camille Flammarion, *Dreams of an Astronomer*, 1923
Jonathan Shackleton

Though the Masonic (or quasi-Masonic) plate is genuine, the book was published a year after Shackleton's death. Shackleton was initiated into the Freemasons on 9 July, 1901, just before the departure of *Discovery*; he joined the Navy Lodge. He was also a Founder Member of the Old Alleynian Lodge, No. 4165; in the printed 'Summons' for the Consecration Meeting on 14 December 1920 his name is printed as a Founder Member [Information from Mr. Patrick Darby]. Shackleton was greatly advantaged in South America by his Masonic connections.

199 **The Union Flag placed on Sir Ernest Shackleton's coffin**
Cotton
99 x 180
Hon. Alexandra Shackleton, currently on loan to Dulwich College
Provenance: John Quiller Rowett; Mrs. Helen Carpenter; presented to the Hon. Alexandra Shackleton, 1997

This flag may be seen in the photograph of the coffin lying in the Lutheran church at Grytviken.

200 **'Our Farewell to the Boss'**
George Wilkins' photograph with members of the *Quest* expedition at Shackleton's grave at Grytviken cemetery, 6 May 1922
14 x 20.4
Private collection

201 **The Memorial Cairn at Grytviken Harbour, South Georgia**
Photograph by A. Saunders
30 x 37
Dulwich College, the gift of the Hon. Alexandra Shackleton

202 **Memorial Service (or Funeral Service) Photographs of Ernest Shackleton, Montevideo, 14 February 1922**
Private collection

(Titles and notes transcribed from back of original photographs)

1. **Sir Ernest's body arriving from the Military Hospital at the British Church, Holy Trinity.**

2. **The body being removed from the British Church after the funeral service.**

3. **The body being placed on the gun carriage.**

4. **The body being placed on the gun carriage.**

5. **The body being placed on the gun carriage.**

6. **Departure from British church on way to S. S. *Woodville*.**

202.7

7. **Procession en route up Calle Treinta y Tres.**

8. **Procession passing along Calle 25 May. Troops are here seen presenting arms.**

9. **Procession on esplanade, nearing the S. S. *Woodville*.**

10. **Arrival of gun carriage carrying the body alongside the S. S. *Woodville*.**

11. **Dr. J. Buero, Uruguayan Minister of Foreign Affairs, speaking prior to body being placed in hold of S. S. *Woodville*.**

12. **British Minister, Edward Hope Vere speaking. Minister of Foreign Affairs, Uruguay.**

13. **Placing body in hold of S. S. *Woodville*.**

14. **The staff of the Hospital at Montevideo.** In centre shorter of the two men is Capt. Hussey who gave up the Expedition to take the body to Grytviken. The nurses kept fresh flowers on his coffin daily.

15. **Sir Ernest's body was guarded by these soldiers for twenty-one days and nights at hospital in Montevideo** while waiting for a whaler to take his body to South Georgia for burial in the little Cemetery at Grytviken (the whaling station).

The date of this Memorial Service (or Funeral) was what would have been Shackleton's forty-eighth birthday. M. & J. Fisher, *Shackleton*, pp. 480–481, quote from Edward Hope Vere, the British Chargé d'Affaires, who sent this report to Lord Curzon at the Foreign Office:

> After the benediction had been pronounced and during the playing of the 'Dead March in Saul', twenty members of the Ex-Service Clubs of Montevideo and Buenos Aires, many of whom held His Majesty's Commission during the war, shouldered the coffin, which was draped in the folds of the Uruguayan flag and the Union Jack and crowned with the wreath placed upon it... on behalf of His Majesty the King and His Majesty's Government.

202.3

At the door of the church the coffin was placed upon the gun-carriage, while a squadron of the famous Uruguayan Cavalry Regiment... known as the 'Blandengues de Artigas', presented arms and then formed in double file as a Guard of Honour on both sides of the gun-carriage and funeral procession, and the fortress of Montevideo fired minute guns. The Uruguayan wreath and those of Shackleton's family were then placed upon and around the coffin, the other being borne in the procession by ex-Officers in His Majesty's Army.

Opposite the English Club, Doctor Buero, the Uruguayan Minister for Foreign Affairs, accompanied by General Sebastian Buquet, the Uruguayan Minister of War and Marine, and General da Costa, Chief of the Uruguayan General Staff, joined the procession, the streets being lined on both sides by troops with reversed arms and all flags half-masted in sign of mourning. Doctor Buero drew my attention to the sympathetic attitude of the large crowd of spectators and to the fact that eighteen hundred troops had been paraded to do honour to Shackleton and as a demonstration of sympathy with Great Britain.

At the landing stage his Excellency formally handed over the remains to me in an eloquent speech... Shackleton's coffin was then carried on board the British steamer 'Woodville', which left this morning at six a.m. for South Georgia, being escorted to the limit of Uruguayan territorial waters by the cruiser 'Uruguay', which then returned to this port after firing a salute.

203 Bronze Memorial Tablet
A Token of Fraternal Affection from Old Alleynians in the River Plate. February 1922.
Photograph, 17.5 x 23.5
Dulwich College

See the essay above.

204 St. Paul's Cathedral
A Service in Memory of Sir Ernest Shackleton. Thursday, March 2nd, 1922.
6 pp.
Private collection

The Service was taken by Dean Inge, and included Shackleton's favourite 23rd Psalm and the hymn 'Eternal Father, strong to save', about 'those in peril on the sea' and the Spirit that originally brooded over the 'angry tumult' of the waters.

205 Charles Sargeant Jagger, M.C., A.R.A. (1885–1934)
The National Memorial Statue to Sir Ernest Shackleton
Photograph (taken in the artist's studio) of the statue now in a niche at the Royal Geographical Society, Kensington Gore, London
Private Collection

Jagger learnt silver-engraving with Mappin and Webb, and studied at the Sheffield School of Art and the Royal College of Art. His more famous works include the Artillery Monument at Hyde Park Corner, the G. W. R. Memorial at Paddington and the British War Memorial to Belgium at Brussels. He was elected A.R.A. in 1926.

The Memorial was unveiled in front of the new Royal Geographical Society building by the Marquess of Zetland on 9 January 1932. The Master of Dulwich College, the Captain of the School and Sir Clement Hindley, K.C.I.E., representing the Alleyn Club, were present.

ACKNOWLEDGEMENTS

QUOTATIONS:

Quotations made from:
Diary of Harry McNeish, by kind permission of the Alexander Turnbull Library, National Library of New Zealand, Wellington;
Diary of Thomas Hans Orde-Lees, by kind permission of Dartmouth College Library, Hanover, New Hampshire;
Shackleton and Fisher papers, by kind permission of the Scott Polar Research Institute, Cambridge.

Photographs by Frank Hurley lent and reproduced by kind permission of the Royal Geographical Society Picture Library, who have held in their collection the original glass plate negatives from this expedition since 1929.

Photographs supplied by the Picture Library, Scott Polar Research Institute, Cambridge are reproduced by kind permission of the Institute.

PICTURE CREDITS

Rights are reserved on all photographs. We are grateful for the generosity of private owners in allowing reproduction of works in their possession. Images are listed by page number: © All Hallows PCC, 147 (left); © Thomas Binnie Jr., 28, 29; © British Library, 45, 46 (left); © Christie's Images 69 (right), 72, 100, 117, 118, 119, 121; © Dulwich College (photographs by Richard Riddick), cover, 42, 44, 46 (right), 49–50, 57, 64, 67, 68 (right), 75, 78, 80 (right), 82, 111 (right), 129, 141; © Andy Fletcher, 52; © Hampshire Council Museums Service, 116, 123, 124; © National Maritime Museum, 152 (left); © Stephen Pugh, Dulwich College, 51, 53; Royal Collection, 99 (bottom) © 2000 Her Majesty the Queen; © Royal Geographical Society Picture Library, 24, 51 (right), 91, 92, 95, 96, 98, 99, 103, 106, 107, 110 (top), 125, 126, 128, 131–140 (inclusive); © Science Museum, 74; © Scott Polar Research Institute Picture Library, 10, 11, 12, 13, 26, 31, 32, 34, 36, 38, 60, 69, 80 (left), 102, 108–9, 112, 113, 120, 122, 154, 155; © Karl Jan Skontorp, 23; © Maria Stenzel/National Geographic Society Image Collection, 2; © Stephen Venables, 4, 6, 7, 8; © Elke Walford, Hamburg, 40.

EXHIBITION SOUNDTRACK

Produced by Chris Russell at the Natural History Museum, London. Wildlife sounds provided by courtesy of the British Library National Sound Archive.
Sponsored by Mars (UK).

CURATOR'S THANKS

Dr. Jan Piggott (Keeper of Archives at Dulwich College), Curator of the Exhibition and the Editor of this volume, would like to thank the following and many others most warmly for their generous and friendly help:

Johnny Van Haeften, George Loudon.

At Dulwich College, Mary Able, John Bardell, Barry Bartlett, Marianne Bradnock, Paul Fletcher, Colin Haggis, Thierry Henrot, Austin Johnston, Jim Keenan, Iona Meek, Katie Millis, Allan Ronald, Will Skinner (Bursar), Martin Tiffin, Terry Walsh, Peter Wilks.

Tom Lamb and Nick Lambourn of Christie's.

The Committee of the James Caird Society.

Giles Bergel, Bob Burton, Michael Gilkes, Jonathan Shackleton, Ann Shirley (Savours).

William Mills (Librarian), Bob Headland (Archivist), and Philippa Smith (Picture Librarian) at the Scott Polar Research Institute; Valerie Mattingley of the National Geographic Society; Andrew Tatham (Keeper) and Joanna Scadden (Picture Librarian) at the Royal Geographical Society; David Spence (Exhibition Projects Director), Sian Flynn, Jane Holmes, Avril Scott, Lorraine Boden, Mac Pritchard, Mary-Jane Holton of the National Maritime Museum; Hugh Roberts (Surveyor of the Queen's Works of Art) and Caroline de Guitaut of the Royal Collection; Giles Clarke (Head of Exhibitions and Education) of the Natural History Museum; Peter Fitzgerald of the Science Museum; Alf Longhurst of Resource; Clive Dunnico (Warden and Secretary) of the Browning Settlement; Anne Rose and the staff of the British Library; Alan Bell and the staff of the London Library; the Rev. Brian Birchmore, All Hallows Church; Stephen Locke and Suzanne Foster of Hampshire Museums and Hampshire Record Office.

Bill Ronald and Graham Storey of Mars (UK); Stuart Leggatt of Sotheran's; Ben Burdett of Atlas Limited Editions; Margaret Battley of Battley Bros.

The late Harding Dunnett, Founder and Chairman of the James Caird Society, for his enthusiasm, endless curiosity and genial knowledge, and for his book *Shackleton's Boat* (1996). Roland Huntford for his magnificent *Shackleton* (1985), and his distinguished predecessors as biographers of Shackleton, Hugh Robert Mill (1923) and Margery and James Fisher (1957).

The interest, practical help and encouragement given by the Hon. Alexandra Shackleton have been absolute. The support of Graham Able, the Master of Dulwich College, has been staunch.

SPONSORSHIP

The Chairman of the Board of Governors of Dulwich College, Lord Butler of Brockwell, G.C.B., C.V.O., and the Board of Governors wish to thank the following:

for major sponsorship of the Exhibition,
 Messrs. Christie's;

for major sponsorship of this catalogue,
 Deborah and Forrest Mars, Mclean, Virginia.

They also wish to thank the following for most generous personal donations towards setting up the exhibition:

The Earl of Chichester
The Lady Shackleton
The Hon. Alexandra Shackleton

John Blackborow
Dr. Harvey Blustain
Trevor Cornford
Roger Croucher
Patrick Darby
Mrs Monica Dunnett
 and the family of the late Harding Dunnett
Alan Farrow
John Harper
Sir John Harvey-Jones
Meredith Hooper
George Loudon
Michael B. McNamara
John and Elizabeth Maggs
Margot Morrell
Edward Pearce
Rudy Ruggles
Martin Sanderson
Jonathan Shackleton
Neil M. Silverman
Michael Smith
Robert B. Stephenson
Johnny and Sarah Van Haeften
Lynette Wheeler
Christopher Wain
Royden Woodford

for most generous donations from Trusts or institutions:

The James Caird Society
The Government of South Georgia and the Sandwich Islands
The Old Alleynian Lodge
The Salen Charitable Trust
The United Kingdom Antarctic Heritage Trust

for most generous donations from organisations:

Atlas Editions
Mars (UK) Ltd.
Orient Lines
Messrs. Sotheran's

LENDERS

Her Majesty the Queen

The Earl of Portsmouth

Roderick Dunnett
Veronica Marston
Dr. Jan Piggott
Jonathan Shackleton
Neil M. Silverman
Johnny and Sarah Van Haeften
Dan and Jonolyn Weinstein, Jamestown, New York

Private collections

All Hallows by the Tower, London EC3
Atlas Limited Editions
The British Library
The Browning Settlement
Hampshire County Museums Services
Hampshire County Record Office
Maggs Brothers Ltd.
The National Maritime Museum
Queen's College, London, Harley Street W1
The Royal Geographical Society
The Scott Polar Research Institute, University of Cambridge
The Science Museum